Guy de Maupassant, Henry James, Jonathan Sturges

The odd Number

Thirteen Tales

Guy de Maupassant, Henry James, Jonathan Sturges

The odd Number
Thirteen Tales

ISBN/EAN: 9783337071226

Printed in Europe, USA, Canada, Australia, Japan

Cover: Foto ©ninafisch / pixelio.de

More available books at **www.hansebooks.com**

THE ODD NUMBER

Thirteen Tales

By

Güy de Maupassant

THE TRANSLATION
By JONATHAN STURGES

AN INTRODUCTION
By HENRY JAMES

NEW YORK
HARPER & BROTHERS, FRANKLIN SQUARE
1889

one question they will always be able to ask without getting an immediate answer, so that the little inquiry will retain more or less its triumphant air. "Why should we concern ourselves so much about French literature, when those who produce it concern themselves so little about ours?"

That strong argument will always be in order, especially among those who do not really know how little the French are, as they say, preoccupied with English and American work; and on some occasions it will be supported by the further inquiry: "Is not the very perfection of French literature to-day an exemplary consequence of the fact that its principal exponents stay at home and mind their business — shut their doors and 'take care of' (*soigner*) their form? They don't waste time," it will be added, "in superficial excursions, nor have they any confidence in the lessons that are to be learned beyond the frontier. Watch them a little and you will see plenty of examples of that want of confidence. They accept their own order of things as their limit, and in that order they dig, as we know, very deep. To speak only of fiction, there are multitudes of tales by English and American writers which profess to deal with

French and with Italian life, yet probably not one of which, unless it be George Eliot's 'Romola,' has any verisimilitude or any value for Frenchmen or for Italians. Few indeed are the works of fiction which they on their side have dedicated to the portraiture of the Anglo-Saxon world; and great, doubtless, do they deem the artistic *naïveté* of a race which can content itself with that sort of stuff as a substitute for thoroughness." Thus, it will be seen, the very "perfection" of French literature (which a hundred observers will also of course contest) may, oddly enough, be offered as a reason for having nothing to do with it.

These are the embroilments of a flirtation —an expression which is really the only proper one to apply to our interest in the "sort of stuff" which has enabled such a writer as M. Guy de Maupassant, whose name I have prefixed to these remarks, to be possible. To a serious and well-regulated union with such a writer the American public must, in the nature of things, shrink from pretending; but nothing need prevent it—not even the sense of danger (often, it must be said, much rather an incentive), from enjoying those desultory snatches of intercourse which represent, in the world of books, the broken opportunities of Rosina or Juliet. These young ladies, it is true, eventually went much further, and the situation of the Anglo-Saxon reader, when craning over the creaking fourth or fifth floor balcony of a translation, must be understood as that to which the romance of curiosity would have been restricted if the Guardian and the Nurse—in other words public opinion—had succeeded in keeping the affair within limits. M. de Maupassant is an Almaviva who strums his guitar with the expectation of raising the street, and he performs most skilfully under those windows from which the flower of attention at any price is flung down to him. If he is a capital specimen of the foreign writer with whom the critic has most trouble, there could at the same time be no better exhibition of the force which sets this inquiring, admiring spirit in motion.

The only excuse the critic has for braving the embarrassments I have mentioned is that he wishes to perform a work of recommendation, and indeed there is no profit in talking, in English, of M. de Maupassant unless it be in the sense of recommending him. One should never go out of one's way to differ, and translation, interpretation, the business of adjusting to another medium, are a going out of one's way. Silence is the best disapproval, and to take people up, with an earnest grip, only to put them down, is to add to the vain gesticulation of the human scene. That reader will therefore be most intelligent who, if he does not leave M. de Maupassant quite alone, makes him a present, as it were, of the conditions. My purpose was to enumerate these, but I shall not accomplish it properly if I fail to recognize that they are manifold.

The first of them to be mentioned is doubtless that he came into the literary world, as he himself has related, under the protection of the great Flaubert. This was but a dozen years ago, for Guy de Maupassant belongs, among the distinguished Frenchmen of his period, to the new generation. His celebrity has been gathered in a short career, and his experience, which, in certain ways, suggests the helping hand of time, in a rapid life, inasmuch as he was born in 1850. These things go fast in France, and there is already a newer generation still, with its dates and its notabilities; but we need scarcely yet open a parenthesis for the so-called *décadents:* they have produced no talent that seems particularly alive

—to do so would indeed be a disloyalty to their name. Besides the link of the same literary ideal, Gustave Flaubert had with his young pupil a strong community of local sense—the sap of the rich old Norman country was in the veins of both. It is not too much to say that there is a large element in Maupassant that the reader will care for in proportion as he has a kindly impression of the large, bountiful Norman land, with its abbeys and its nestling farms, its scented hedges and hard white roads, where the Sunday blouse of the rustic is picked out in color, its succulent domestic life, and its canny and humorous peasantry. There is something in the accumulated heritage of such a province which may well have fed the imagination of an artist whose vision was to be altogether of this life.

That is another of M. de Maupassant's conditions: what is clearest to him is the immitigability of our mortal predicament, with its occasional beguilements and its innumerable woes. Flaubert would have been sorry to blur this sharpness, and indeed he ministered to it in helping to place his young friend in possession of a style which completely reflects it. Guy de Maupassant, from his own account (in the preface to

"Pierre et Jean"), devoted much time to the moral that to prove that you have a first-rate talent you must have a first-rate style. He therefore learned to write, and acquired an instrument which emits no uncertain sound. He is wonderfully concise and direct, yet at the same time it would be difficult to characterize more vividly. To have color and be sober with it is an ideal, and this ideal M. de Maupassant constantly touches. The complete possession of his instrument has enabled him to attack a great variety of subjects—usually within rigid limits of space. He has accepted the necessity of being brief, and has made brevity very full, through making it an energetic selection. He has published less than half a dozen novels and more than a hundred tales, and it is upon his tales that his reputation will mainly rest. The short tale is infinitely relished in France, which can show, in this form, an array of masterpieces; and no small part of Maupassant's success, I think, comes from his countrymen's pride in seeing him add to a collection which is already a national glory. He has done so, as I say, by putting selection really upon its mettle— by going, in every picture, straight to the strongest ingredients, and to them alone.

The turn of his mind has helped him to do this, an extraordinary perceptive apparatus of the personal, material, immediate sort. M. de Maupassant takes his stand on everything that solicits the sentient creature who lives in his senses; gives the impression of the active, independent observer who is ashamed of none of his faculties, describes what he sees, renders, with a rare reproduction of tone, what he hears, and is more anxious to see and to hear than to make sure, in advance, of propping up some particular theory of things. He has indeed a theory to the effect that they are pretty bad, but practically the air of truth in the given case is almost never sacrificed to it. His strong, hard, cynical, slightly cruel humor can scarcely be called a theory; what one may say of this rather is that his drollery is a direct emanation from the facts, and especially from the rural facts, which he knows with extraordinary knowledge. His most brilliantly clever tales deal with the life, pervaded, for the most part, by a strong smell of the barn-yard and the wine-shop, of the Norman cottage and market-place. Such a little picture as "La Ficelle" ("The Piece of String") is a pure gem, so caught in the fact are the whimsicalities of the thick-witted rustic world.

For the last ten years M. de Maupassant has contributed an almost weekly *nouvelle* to some Parisian sheet which has allowed him a luxurious liberty. They have been very unequal, too numerous, and occasionally bad enough to be by an inferior hand (an inevitable accident, in copious production); but they have contained an immense element of delightful work. Taken all together, they are full of life (of life as the author conceives it, of course—he is far from having taken its measure in all directions), and between the lines of them we seem to read of that partly pleasant and wholly modern invention, a roving existence in which, for art, no impression is wasted. M. de Maupassant travels, explores, navigates, shoots, goes up in balloons, and writes. He treats of the north and of the south, evidently makes "copy" of everything that happens to him, and, in the interest of such copy and such happenings, ranges from Etretat to the depths of Algeria. Lately he has given signs of adding a new cord to his bow—a silver cord, of intenser vibration. His two last novels, "Pierre et Jean" and "Fort comme la Mort," deal with shades of feeling and delicacies of experience to which he had shown himself rather a stranger. They are the work of an older man, and of a man who has achieved the feat of keeping his talent fresh when other elements have turned stale. In default of other convictions it may still, for the artist, be an adequate working faith to turn out something fine. Guy de Maupassant is a striking illustration of this curious truth and of the practical advantage of having a first-rate ability. Such a gift may produce surprises in the mere exercise of its natural health. The dogmatist is never safe with it.

Henry James

LONDON, *August 6, 1889.*

I.
HAPPINESS.

HAPPINESS.

It was tea-time before the appearance of the lamps. The villa commanded the sea; the sun, which had disappeared, had left the sky all rosy from his passing—rubbed, as it were, with gold-dust; and the Mediterranean, without a ripple, without a shudder, smooth, still shining under the dying day, seemed like a huge and polished metal plate.

Far off to the right the jagged mountains outlined their black profile on the paled purple of the west.

We talked of love, we discussed that old subject, we said again the things which we had said already very often. The sweet melancholy of the twilight made our words slower, caused a tenderness to waver in our souls; and that word, "love," which came back ceaselessly, now pronounced by a strong man's voice, now uttered by the frail-toned voice of a woman, seemed to fill the little *salon*, to flutter there like a bird, to hover there like a spirit.

Can one remain in love for several years in succession?

"Yes," maintained some.

"No," affirmed others.

We distinguished cases, we established limitations, we cited examples; and all, men and women, filled with rising and troubling memories, which they could not quote, and which mounted to their lips, seemed moved, and talked of that common, that sovereign thing, the tender and mysterious union of two beings, with a profound emotion and an ardent interest.

But all of a sudden some one, whose eyes had been fixed upon the distance, cried out:

"Oh! Look down there; what is it?"

On the sea, at the bottom of the horizon, loomed up a mass, gray, enormous and confused.

The women had risen from their seats, and without understanding, looked at this surprising thing which they had never seen before.

Some one said:

"It is Corsica! You see it so two or three times a year, in certain exceptional conditions of the atmosphere, when the air is perfectly clear, and it is not concealed by those mists of sea-fog which always veil the distances."

We distinguished vaguely the mountain ridges, we thought we recognized the snow of their summits. And every one remained surprised, troubled, almost terrified, by this sudden apparition of a world, by this phantom risen from the sea. Maybe that those who, like Columbus, went away across undiscovered oceans had such strange visions as this.

Then said an old gentleman who had not yet spoken:

"See here: I knew in that island which raises itself before us, as if in person to answer what we said, and to recall to me a singular memory—I knew, I say, an admirable case of love which was true, of love which, improbably enough, was happy.

"Here it is—

"Five years ago I made a journey in Corsica. That savage island is more unknown and more distant from us than America, even though you see it sometimes from the very coasts of France, as we have done to-day.

"Imagine a world which is still chaos, imagine a storm of mountains separated by narrow ravines where torrents roll; not a single plain, but immense waves of granite, and giant undulations of earth covered with brushwood or with high forests of chestnut-trees and pines. It is a virgin soil, uncultivated, desert, although you sometimes make out a village, like a heap of rocks, on the summit of a mountain. No culture, no industries, no art. One never meets here with a morsel of carved wood, or a bit of sculptured stone, never the least reminder that the ancestors of these people had any taste, whether rude or refined, for gracious and beautiful things. It is this which strikes you the most in their superb and hard country: their hereditary indifference to that search for seductive forms which is called Art.

"Italy, where every palace, full of masterpieces, is a masterpiece itself; Italy, where marble, wood, bronze, iron, metals, and precious stones attest man's genius, where the smallest old things which lie about in the ancient houses reveal that divine care for grace — Italy is for us the sacred country which we love, because she shows to us and proves to us the struggle, the grandeur, the power, and the triumph of the intelligence which creates.

"And, face to face with her, the savage Corsica has remained exactly as in her earliest days. A man lives there in his rude house, indifferent to everything which does not concern his own bare existence or his family feuds. And he has retained the vices and the virtues of savage races; he is violent, malignant, sanguinary without a thought of remorse, but also hospitable, generous, devoted, simple, opening his door to passers-by, and giving his faithful friendship in return for the least sign of sympathy.

"So, for a month, I had been wandering over this magnificent island with the sensation that I was at the end of the world. No more inns, no taverns, no roads. You gain by mule-paths hamlets hanging up, as it were, on a mountain-side, and commanding tortuous abysses whence of an evening you hear rising the steady sound, the dull and deep voice, of the torrent. You knock at the doors of the houses. You ask a shelter for the night and something to live on till the morrow. And you sit down at the humble board, and you sleep under the humble roof, and in the morning you press the extended hand of your host, who has guided you as far as the outskirts of the village.

"Now, one night, after ten hours' walking, I reached a little dwelling quite by itself at the bottom of a narrow valley which was about to throw itself into the sea a league farther on. The two steep slopes of the mountain, covered with brush, with fallen rocks, and with great trees, shut in this lamentably sad ravine like two sombre walls.

"Around the cottage were some vines, a little garden, and, farther off, several large chestnut-trees—enough to live on; in fact, a fortune for this poor country.

"'The woman who received me was old, severe, and neat—exceptionally so. The man, seated on a straw chair, rose to salute me, then sat down again without saying a word. His companion said to me:

"'Excuse him; he is deaf now. He is eighty-two years old.'

"She spoke the French of France. I was surprised.

"I asked her:

"'You are not of Corsica?'

"She answered:

"'No; we are from the Continent. But we have lived here now fifty years.'

"A feeling of anguish and of fear seized me at the thought of those fifty years passed in this gloomy hole, so far from the cities where human beings dwell. An old shepherd returned, and we began to eat the only dish there was for dinner, a thick soup in which potatoes, lard, and cabbages had been boiled together.

"When the short repast was finished, I went and sat down before the door, my heart pinched by the melancholy of the mournful landscape, wrung by that distress which sometimes seizes travellers on certain sad evenings, in certain desolate places. It seems that everything is near its ending—existence, and the universe itself. You perceive sharply the dreadful misery of life, the isolation of every one, the nothingness of all things, and the black loneliness of the heart which nurses itself and deceives itself with dreams until the hour of death.

"The old woman rejoined me, and, tortured by that curiosity which ever lives at the bottom of the most resigned of souls:

"'So you come from France?' said she.

"'Yes; I'm travelling for pleasure.'

"'You are from Paris, perhaps?'

"'No, I am from Nancy.'

"It seemed to me that an extraordinary emotion agitated her. How I saw, or rather how I felt it, I do not know.

"She repeated, in a slow voice:

"'You are from Nancy?'

"The man appeared in the door, impassible, like all the deaf.

"She resumed:

"'It doesn't make any difference. He can't hear.'

"Then, at the end of several seconds:

"'So you know people at Nancy?'

"'Oh yes, nearly everybody.'

"'The family of Sainte-Allaize?'

"'Yes, very well; they were friends of my father.'

"'What are you called?'

"I told her my name. She regarded me fixedly, then said, in that low voice which is roused by memories:

"'Yes, yes; I remember well. And the Brisemares, what has become of them?'

"'They are all dead.'

"'Ah! And the Sirmonts, do you know them?'

"'Yes, the last of the family is a general.'

"Then she said, trembling with emotion, with anguish, with I do not know what, feeling confused, powerful, and holy, with I do not know how great a need to confess, to tell all, to talk of those things which she had hitherto kept shut in the bottom of her heart, and to speak of those people whose name distracted her soul:

"'Yes, Henri de Sirmont. I know him well. He is my brother.'

"And I lifted my eyes at her, aghast with surprise. And all of a sudden my memory of it came back.

"It had caused, once, a great scandal among the nobility of Lorraine. A young girl, beautiful and rich, Suzanne de Sirmont, had run away with an under-officer in the regiment of hussars commanded by her father.

"He was a handsome fellow, the son of a peasant, but he carried his blue dolman very well, this soldier who had captivated his colonel's daughter. She had seen him, noticed him, fallen in love with him, doubtless while watching the squadrons filing by. But how she had got speech of him, how they had managed to see one another, to hear from one another; how she had dared to let him understand she loved him—that was never known.

"Nothing was divined, nothing suspected. One night when the soldier had just finished his time of service, they disappeared together. Her people looked for them in vain.

They never received tidings, and they considered her as dead.

"So I found her in this sinister valley.

"Then in my turn I took up the word:

"'Yes, I remember well. You are Mademoiselle Suzanne.'

"She made the sign 'yes,' with her head. Tears fell from her eyes. Then with a look showing me the old man motionless on the threshold of his hut, she said:

"'That is he.'

"And I understood that she loved him yet, that she still saw him with her bewitched eyes.

"I asked:

"'Have you at least been happy?'

"She answered with a voice which came from her heart:

"'Oh yes! very happy. He has made me very happy. I have never regretted.'

"I looked at her, sad, surprised, astounded by the sovereign strength of love! That rich young lady had followed this man, this peasant. She was become herself a peasant woman. She had made for herself a life without charm, without luxury, without delicacy of any kind, she had stooped to simple customs. And she loved him yet. She was become the wife of a rustic, in a cap, in a cloth skirt. Seated on a straw-bottomed chair, she ate from an earthen-ware dish, at a wooden table, a soup of potatoes and of cabbages with lard. She slept on a mattress by his side.

"She had never thought of anything but of him. She had never regretted her jewels, nor her fine dresses, nor the elegancies of life, nor the perfumed warmth of the chambers hung with tapestry, nor the softness of the down-beds where the body sinks in for repose. She had never had need of anything but him; provided he was there, she desired nothing.

"Still young, she had abandoned life and the world and those who had brought her up, and who had loved her. She had come, alone with him, into this savage valley. And he had been everything to her, all that one desires, all that one dreams of, all that one waits for without ceasing, all that one hopes for without end. He had filled her life with happiness from the one end to the other.

"She could not have been more happy.

"And all the night, listening to the hoarse breathing of the old soldier stretched on his pallet beside her who had followed him so far, I thought of this strange and simple adventure, of this happiness so complete, made of so very little.

"And I went away at sunrise, after having pressed the hands of that aged pair."

The story-teller was silent. A woman said:

"All the same, she had ideals which were too easily satisfied, needs which were too primitive, requirements which were too simple. She could only have been a fool."

Another said, in a low, slow voice, "What matter! she was happy."

And down there at the end of the horizon, Corsica was sinking into the night, returning gently into the sea, blotting out her great shadow, which had appeared as if in person to tell the story of those two humble lovers who were sheltered by her coasts.

II.

A COWARD.

A COWARD.

In society they called him "the handsome Signoles." His name was Viscount Gontran Joseph de Signoles.

An orphan and the possessor of a sufficient fortune, as the saying goes, he cut a dash. He had a fine figure and bearing, enough conversation to make people credit him with cleverness, a certain natural grace, an air of nobility and of pride, a gallant mustache, and a gentle eye—a thing which pleases women.

In the drawing-rooms he was in great request, much sought after as a partner for the waltz; and he inspired among men that smiling hatred which they always cherish for others of an energetic figure. He passed a happy and tranquil life, in a comfort of mind which was most complete. It was known that he was a good fencer, and as a pistol-shot even better.

"If ever I fight a duel," said he, "I shall choose pistols. With that weapon I am sure of killing my man."

Now, one night, having accompanied two young ladies, his friends, escorted by their husbands, to the theatre, he invited them all after the play to take an ice at Tortoni's. They had been there for several minutes, when he perceived that a gentleman seated at a neighboring table was staring obstinately at one of his companions. She seemed put out, uneasy, lowered her head. At last she said to her husband:

"There is a man who is looking me out of countenance. I do not know him; do you?"

The husband, who had seen nothing, raised his eyes, but declared:

"No, not at all."

The young lady continued, half smiling, half vexed

"It is very unpleasant; that man is spoiling my ice."

Her husband shrugged his shoulders:

"Bast! don't pay any attention to it. If we had to occupy ourselves about every insolent fellow that we meet we should never have done."

But the viscount had risen brusquely. He could not allow that this stranger should spoil an ice which he had offered. It was to him that this insult was addressed, because it was through him and on his account that his friends had entered this café. So the matter concerned him only.

He advanced towards the man and said to him:

"You have, sir, a manner of looking at those ladies which I cannot tolerate. I beg of you to be so kind as to cease from this insistence."

The other answered:

"You are going to mind your own business, curse you."

The viscount said, with close-pressed teeth:

"Take care, sir, you will force me to pass bounds."

The gentleman answered but one word, a

foul word, which rang from one end of the café to the other, and, like a metal spring, caused every guest to execute a sudden movement. All those whose backs were turned wheeled round; all the others raised their heads; three waiters pivoted upon their heels like tops; the two ladies at the desk gave a jump, then turned round their whole bodies from the waists up, as if they had been two automata obedient to the same crank.

A great silence made itself felt. Then, on a sudden, a dry sound cracked in the air. The viscount had slapped his adversary's face. Every one rose to interfere. Cards were exchanged between the two.

When the viscount had reached home he paced his room for several minutes with great, quick strides. He was too much agitated to reflect at all. One single idea was hovering over his mind—"a duel"—without arousing in him as yet an emotion of any sort. He had done that which he ought to have done; he had shown himself to be that which he ought to be. People would talk about it, they would praise him, they would congratulate him. He repeated in a loud voice, speaking as one speaks when one's thoughts are very much troubled :

" What a brute the fellow was !"

Then he sat down and began to reflect. He must find seconds, the first thing in the morning. Whom should he choose? He thought over those men of his acquaintance who had the best positions, who were the most celebrated. He finally selected the Marquis de la Tour-Noire, and the Colonel Bourdin, a nobleman and a soldier. Very good indeed! Their names would sound well in the papers. He perceived that he was thirsty, and he drank, one after another, three glasses of water; then he began again to walk up and down the room. He felt himself full of energy. If he blustered a little, if he showed himself resolute at all points, if he demanded rigorous and dangerous conditions, if he insisted on a serious duel, very serious, terrible, his opponent would probably withdraw and make apologies.

He picked up the card which he had

pulled out of his pocket and thrown on the table, and he reread it with a single glance. He had already done so at the café and in the cab, by the glimmer of every street lamp, on his way home. "Georges Lamil, 51 Rue Moncey." Nothing more.

He examined these assembled letters, which seemed to him mysterious, and full of a confused meaning. Georges Lamil? Who was this man? What had he been about? Why had he stared at that woman in such a way? Was it not revolting that a stranger, an unknown, should so come and trouble your life, all on a sudden, simply because he had been pleased to fix his eyes insolently upon a woman that you knew? And the viscount repeated yet again, in a loud voice:

"What a brute!"

Then he remained motionless, upright, thinking, his look ever planted on the card. A rage awoke in him against this piece of paper, an anger full of hate in which was mixed a strange, uneasy feeling. It was stupid, this whole affair! He took a little penknife which lay open to his hand, and pricked it into the middle of the printed name, as if he had poniarded some one.

However, they must fight! He considered himself as indeed the insulted party. And, having thus the right, should he choose the pistol or the sword? With the sword he risked less; but with the pistol he had the chance of making his adversary withdraw. It is very rare that a duel with swords proves mortal, a mutual prudence preventing the combatants from engaging near enough for the point of a rapier to enter very deep. With the pistol he risked his life seriously; but he might also come out of the affair with all the honors of the situation, and without going so far as an actual meeting.

He said:

"I must be firm. He will be afraid."

The sound of his voice made him tremble, and he looked about him. He felt himself very nervous. He drank another glass of water, then began to undress himself to go to bed.

As soon as he was in bed, he blew out the light and shut his eyes.

He thought:

"I've got all day to-morrow to attend to my affairs. I'd better sleep first so as to be calm."

He was very warm under the bedclothes, but he could not manage to doze off. He turned and twisted, remained five minutes on his back, then placed himself on his left side, then rolled over to his right.

He was still thirsty. He got up again to drink. Then an anxiety seized him:

"Shall I be afraid?"

Why did his heart fall to beating so madly at each of the well-known noises of his chamber? When the clock was about to strike, the little grinding sound of the spring which stands erect, caused him to give a start; and for several seconds after that he was obliged to open his mouth to breathe, he remained so much oppressed.

He set himself to reasoning with himself upon the possibility of this thing:

"Shall I be afraid?"

No, certainly not, he would not be afraid, because he was resolute to go to the end, because he had his will firmly fixed to fight and not to tremble. But he felt so deeply troubled that he asked himself:

"Can a man be afraid in spite of him?"

And this doubt invaded him, this uneasiness, this dread. If some force stronger than his will, if some commanding, and irresistible power should conquer him, what would happen? Yes, what could happen? He should certainly appear upon the field, since he willed to do it. But if he trembled? But if he fainted? And he thought of his situation, of his reputation, of his name.

And a curious necessity seized him on a sudden to get up again and look at himself in the mirror. He relit his candle. When he perceived his face reflected in the polished glass he hardly recognized himself, and it seemed to him that he had never seen this man before. His eyes appeared enormous; and he was pale, surely he was pale, very pale.

He remained upright before the mirror. He put out his tongue as if to test the state of his health, and all on a sudden this thought entered into him after the fashion of a bullet:

"The day after to-morrow, at this time, I shall perhaps be dead."

And his heart began again to beat furiously.

"The day after to-morrow, at this time, I shall perhaps be dead. This person before me, this 'I' which I see in this glass, will exist no longer. What! here I am, I am looking at myself, I feel myself to live, and in twenty-four hours I shall be laid to rest upon this couch, dead, my eyes shut, cold, inanimate, gone."

He turned towards his bed and he distinctly saw himself extended on the back in the same sheets which he had just left. He had the hollow face which dead men have, and that slackness to the hands which will never stir more.

So he grew afraid of his bed, and, in order not to look at it again, he passed into his smoking-room. He took a cigar mechanically, lit it, and again began to walk the room. He was cold; he went towards the bell to wake his valet; but he stopped, his hand lifted towards the bell-rope:

"That fellow will see that I am afraid."

And he did not ring, he made the fire himself. When his hands touched anything they trembled slightly, with a nervous shaking. His head wandered; his troubled thoughts became fugitive, sudden, melancholy; an intoxication seized on his spirit as if he had been drunk.

And ceaselessly he asked himself:

"What shall I do? What will become of me?"

His whole body vibrated, jerky tremblings ran over it; he got up, and approaching the window, he opened the curtains.

The day was coming, a day of summer. The rosy sky made rosy the city, the roofs, and the walls. A great fall of tenuous light, like a caress from the rising sun, enveloped the awakened world; and, with this glimmer, a hope gay, rapid, brutal, seized on the heart of the viscount! Was he mad to let himself be so struck down by fear, before anything had even been decided, before his seconds had seen those of this Georges Lamil, before he yet knew if he was going to fight at all?

He made his toilet, dressed himself, and left the house with a firm step.

He repeated to himself, while walking:

"I must be decided, very decided. I must prove that I am not afraid."

His seconds, the marquis and the colonel, put themselves at his disposition, and after having pressed his hands energetically, discussed the conditions of the meeting.

The colonel asked:

"You want a serious duel?"

The viscount answered:

"Very serious."

The marquis took up the word.

"You insist on pistols?"

"Yes."

"Do you leave us free to settle the rest?"

The viscount articulated with a dry, jerky voice:

"Twenty paces, firing at the word, lifting the arm instead of lowering it. Exchange of shots until some one is badly wounded."

The colonel declared, in a satisfied tone:

"Those are excellent conditions. You are a good shot; the chances are all in your favor."

And they separated. The viscount returned home to wait for them. His agitation, which had been temporarily calmed, was now increasing with every moment. He felt along his arms, along his legs, in his chest, a kind of quivering, a kind of continuous vibration; he could not stay in one place, neither sitting down nor standing up. He had no longer a trace of moisture in his mouth, and he made at every instant a noisy movement of the tongue as if to unglue it from his palate.

He tried to take his breakfast, but he could not eat. Then he thought of drinking in order to give himself courage, and had a decanter of rum brought him, from which he gulped down, one after the other, six little glasses.

A warmth, like a burn, seized on him. It was followed as soon by a giddiness of the soul. He thought:

"I know the way. Now it will go all right."

But at the end of an hour he had emptied the decanter, and his state of agitation was become again intolerable. He felt a wild necessity to oll upon the ground, to cry, to bite. Evening fell.

The sound of the door-bell caused him such a feeling of suffocation that he had not the strength to rise to meet his seconds.

He did not even dare to talk to them any longer—to say "How do you do?" to pronounce a single word, for fear lest they divine all from the alteration in his voice.

The colonel said:

"Everything is settled according to the conditions which you fixed. Your opponent at first insisted on the privileges of the offended party, but he yielded almost immediately, and has agreed to everything. His seconds are two officers.

The viscount said:

"Thank you."

The marquis resumed:

"Excuse us if we only just run in and out, but we've still a thousand things to do. We must have a good doctor, because the duel is not to stop till after some one is badly hit, and you know there's no trifling with bullets. A place must be appointed near some house where we can carry the wounded one of the two, if it is necessary, etc.; it will take us quite two or three hours more."

The viscount articulated a second time:
"Thank you."
The colonel asked:
"You're all right? You're calm?"
"Yes, quite calm, thanks."
The two men retired.

When he felt himself alone again, it seemed to him that he was going mad. His servant having lit the lamps, he sat down before his table to write some letters. After tracing at the top of a page, "This is my Will," he got up again and drew off, feeling incapable of putting two ideas together, of taking a single resolution, of deciding anything at all.

And so he was going to fight a duel! He could no longer escape that. What could be passing within him? He wanted to fight, he had that intention and that resolution firmly fixed; and he felt very plainly that, notwithstanding all the effort of his mind and all the tension of his will, he would not be able to retain strength enough to go as far as the place of the encounter. He tried to fancy the combat, his own attitude, and the bearing of his adversary.

From time to time, his teeth struck against one another in his mouth with a little dry noise. He tried to read, and took up de Châteauvillard's duelling code. Then he asked himself:

"My adversary, has he frequented the shooting-galleries? Is he well known? What's his class? How can I find out?"

He remembered the book by Baron de Vaux upon pistol-shooters, and he searched through it from one end to the other. Georges Lamil was not mentioned. But, however, if the man had not been a good shot, he would not have accepted immediately that dangerous weapon and those conditions, which were mortal.

His pistol-case by Gastinne Renette lay on a little round table. As he passed he opened it and took out one of the pistols, then placed himself as if to shoot, and raised his arm; but he trembled from head to foot, and the barrel shook in all directions.

Then he said:

"It is impossible. I cannot fight like this."

At the end of the barrel he regarded that little hole, black and deep, which spits out death; he thought of dishonor, of the whispers in the clubs, of the laughter in the drawing-rooms, of the disdain of women, of the allusions in the papers, of the insults which would be thrown at him by cowards.

He went on staring at the pistol, and raising the hammer, he suddenly saw a priming glitter beneath it like a little red flame. The pistol had been left loaded, by chance, by oversight. And he experienced from that a confused inexplicable joy.

If in the presence of the other he had not the calm and noble bearing which is fit, he would be lost forever. He would be spotted, marked with a sign of infamy, hunted from society. And he should not have that calm and bold bearing; he knew it, he felt it. And yet he was really brave, because he wanted to fight! He was brave, because—. The thought which just grazed him did not even complete itself in his spirit; but, opening his mouth wide, he brusquely thrust the pistol-barrel into the very bottom of his throat and pressed upon the trigger. . . .

When his valet ran in, attracted by the report, he found him dead, on his back. A jet of blood had spattered the white paper on the table and made a great red stain below the four words :

" This is my Will."

III.

THE WOLF.

THE WOLF.

Here is what the old Marquis d'Arville told us towards the end of St. Hubert's dinner at the house of the Baron des Ravels.

We had killed a stag that day. The marquis was the only one of the guests who had not taken any part in this chase; for he never hunted.

All through that long repast we had talked about hardly anything but the slaughter of animals. The ladies themselves were interested in tales sanguinary and often unlikely, and the orators imitated the attacks and the combats of men against beasts, raised their arms, romanced in a thundering voice.

M. d'Arville talked well, with a certain poetry of style somewhat high-sounding, but full of effect. He must have repeated this story often, for he told it fluently, not hesitating on words, choosing them with skill to produce a picture—

Gentlemen, I have never hunted, neither did my father, nor my grandfather, nor my great-grandfather. This last was the son of a man who hunted more than all of you put together. He died in 1764. I will tell you how.

His name was Jean. He was married, father of that child who became my ancestor, and he lived with his younger brother, François d'Arville, in our castle in Lorraine, in the middle of the forest.

François d'Arville had remained a bachelor for love of the chase.

They both hunted from one end of the year to the other, without repose, without stopping, without fatigue. They loved only that, understood nothing else, talked only of that, lived only for that.

They had at heart that one passion, which was terrible and inexorable. It consumed them, having entirely invaded them, leaving place for no other.

They had given orders that they should not be interrupted in the chase, for any reason whatever. My great-grandfather was born while his father was following a fox, and Jean d'Arville did not stop his pursuit, but he swore: "Name of a name, that rascal there might have waited till after the view-halloo!"

His brother François showed himself still more infatuated. On rising he went to see the dogs, then the horses, then he shot little birds about the castle until the moment for departing to hunt down some great beast.

In the country-side they were called M. le Marquis and M. le Cadet, the nobles then not doing at all like the chance nobility of our time, which wishes to establish an hereditary hierarchy in titles; for the son of a marquis is no more a count, nor the son of a viscount a baron, than the son of a general is a colonel by birth. But the mean vanity of to-day finds profit in that arrangement.

I return to my ancestors.

They were, it seems, immeasurably tall, bony, hairy, violent, and vigorous. The younger, still taller than the older, had a voice so strong that, according to a legend of which he was proud, all the leaves of the forests shook when he shouted.

And when they both mounted to go off to the hunt, that must have been a superb spectacle to see those two giants straddling their huge horses.

Now towards the midwinter of that year, 1764, the frosts were excessive, and the wolves became ferocious.

They even attacked belated peasants, roamed at night about the houses, howled from sunset to sunrise, and depopulated the stables.

And soon a rumor began to circulate. People talked of a colossal wolf, with gray fur, almost white, who had eaten two children, gnawed off a woman's arm, strangled all the dogs of the *garde du pays*, and penetrated without fear into the farm-yards to come snuffling under the doors. The people in the houses affirmed that they had felt his breath, and that it made the flame of the

THE WOLF. 43

lights flicker. And soon a panic ran through all the province. No one dared go out any more after night-fall. The shades seemed haunted by the image of the beast.

The brothers d'Arville resolved to find and kill him, and several times they assembled all the gentlemen of the country to a great hunting.

In vain. They might beat the forests and search the coverts, they never met him. They killed wolves, but not that one. And every night after a *battue*, the beast, as if to avenge himself, attacked some traveller or devoured some one's cattle, always far from the place where they had looked for him.

Finally one night he penetrated into the pig-pen of the Château d'Arville and ate the two finest pigs.

The brothers were inflamed with anger, considering this attack as a bravado of the monster, an insult direct, a defiance. They took their strong blood-hounds used to pursue formidable beasts, and they set off to hunt, their hearts swollen with fury.

From dawn until the hour when the empurpled sun descended behind the great naked trees, they beat the thickets without finding anything.

At last, furious and disconsolate, both were returning, walking their horses along an *allée* bordered with brambles, and they marvelled that their woodcraft should be crossed so by this wolf, and they were seized suddenly with a sort of mysterious fear.

The elder said:

"That beast there is not an ordinary one. You would say it thought like a man."

The younger answered:

"Perhaps we should have a bullet blessed by our cousin, the bishop, or pray some priest to pronounce the words which are needed."

Then they were silent.

Jean continued:

"Look how red the sun is. The great wolf will do some harm to-night."

He had hardly finished speaking when his horse reared; that of François began to kick. A large thicket covered with dead leaves opened before them, and a colossal beast, quite gray, sprang up and ran off across the wood.

Both uttered a kind of groan of joy, and bending over the necks of their heavy horses, they threw them forward with an impulse from all their body, hurling them on at such a pace, exciting them, hurrying them away, maddening them so with the voice, with gesture, and with spur that the strong riders seemed rather to be carrying the heavy beasts between their thighs and to bear them off as if they were flying.

Thus they went, *ventre à terre*, bursting the thickets, cleaving the beds of streams, climbing the hill-sides, descending the gorges, and blowing on the horn with full lungs to attract their people and their dogs.

And now, suddenly, in that mad race, my ancestor struck his forehead against an enormous branch which split his skull; and he fell stark dead on the ground, while his frightened horse took himself off, disappearing in the shade which enveloped the woods.

The cadet of Arville stopped short, leaped to the earth, seized his brother in his arms, and he saw that the brains ran from the wound with the blood.

Then he sat down beside the body, rested the head, disfigured and red, on his knees, and waited, contemplating that immobile face of the elder brother. Little by little a fear invaded him, a strange fear which he had never felt before, the fear of the dark, the fear of solitude, the fear of the deserted wood, and the fear also of the fantastic wolf who had just killed his brother to avenge himself upon them both.

The shadows thickened, the acute cold made the trees crack. François got up, shivering, unable to remain there longer, feeling himself almost growing faint. Nothing was to be heard, neither the voice of the dogs nor the sound of the horns—all was silent along the invisible horizon; and this mournful silence of the frozen night had something about it frightening and strange.

He seized in his colossal hands the great body of Jean, straightened it and laid it across the saddle to carry it back to the château; then he went on his way softly, his mind troubled as if he were drunken, pursued by horrible and surprising images.

And abruptly, in the path which the night

was invading, a great shape passed. It was the beast. A shock of terror shook the hunter; something cold, like a drop of water, glided along his reins, and, like a monk haunted of the devil, he made a great sign of the cross, dismayed at this abrupt return of the frightful prowler. But his eyes fell back upon the inert body laid before him, and suddenly, passing abruptly from fear to anger, he shook with an inordinate rage.

Then he spurred his horse and rushed after the wolf.

He followed it by the copses, the ravines, and the tall trees, traversing woods which he no longer knew, his eyes fixed on the white speck which fled before him through the night now fallen upon the earth.

His horse also seemed animated by a force and an ardor hitherto unknown. It galloped, with out-stretched neck, straight on, hurling against the trees, against the rocks, the head and the feet of the dead man thrown across the saddle. The briers tore out the hair; the brow, beating the huge trunks, spattered them with blood; the spurs tore their ragged coats of bark.

And suddenly the beast and the horseman issued from the forest and rushed into a valley, just as the moon appeared above the mountains. This valley was stony, closed by enormous rocks, without possible issue; and the wolf was cornered and turned round.

François then uttered a yell of joy which the echoes repeated like a rolling of thunder, and he leaped from his horse, his cutlass in his hand.

The beast, with bristling hair, the back arched, awaited him; its eyes glistened like two stars. But, before offering battle, the strong hunter, seizing his brother, seated him on a rock, and, supporting with stones his head, which was no more than a blot of blood, he shouted in the ears as if he was talking to a deaf man, "Look, Jean; look at this!"

Then he threw himself upon the monster. He felt himself strong enough to overturn a mountain, to bruise stones in his hands. The beast tried to bite him, seeking to strike in at his stomach; but he had seized it by the neck, without even using his weapon, and he strangled it gently, listening to the stoppage of the breathings in its throat and the beatings of its heart. And he laughed, rejoicing madly, pressing closer and closer his formidable embrace, crying in a delirium of joy, " Look, Jean, look!" All resistance ceased; the body of the wolf became lax. He was dead.

Then François, taking him up in his arms, carried him off and went and threw him at the feet of the elder brother, repeating, in a tender voice, " There, there, there, my little Jean, see him!"

Then he replaced on the saddle the two bodies one upon the other; and he went his way.

He returned to the château, laughing and crying, like Gargantua at the birth of Pantagruel, uttering shouts of triumph and stamping with joy in relating the death of the beast, and moaning and tearing his beard in telling that of his brother.

And often, later, when he talked again of that day, he said, with tears in his eyes, " If only that poor Jean could have seen me strangle the other, he would have died content, I am sure of it!"

The widow of my ancestor inspired her orphan son with that horror of the chase which has transmitted itself from father to son as far down as myself.

The Marquis d'Arville was silent. Some one asked:

"That story is a legend, isn't it?"

And the story-teller answered:

"I swear to you that it is true from one end to the other."

Then a lady declared, in a little, soft voice:

"All the same, it is fine to have passions like that."

IV.

THE NECKLACE.

THE NECKLACE.

She was one of those pretty and charming girls who are sometimes, as if by a mistake of destiny, born in a family of clerks. She had no dowry, no expectations, no means of being known, understood, loved, wedded, by any rich and distinguished man; and she let herself be married to a little clerk at the Ministry of Public Instruction.

She dressed plainly because she could not dress well, but she was as unhappy as though she had really fallen from her proper station; since with women there is neither caste nor rank; and beauty, grace, and charm act instead of family and birth. Natural fineness, instinct for what is elegant, suppleness of wit, are the sole hierarchy, and make from women of the people the equals of the very greatest ladies.

She suffered ceaselessly, feeling herself born for all the delicacies and all the luxuries. She suffered from the poverty of her dwelling, from the wretched look of the walls, from the worn-out chairs, from the ugliness of the curtains. All those things, of which another woman of her rank would never even have been conscious, tortured her and made her angry. The sight of the little Breton peasant who did her humble house-work aroused in her regrets which were despairing, and distracted dreams. She thought of the silent antechambers hung with Oriental tapestry, lit by tall bronze candelabra, and of the two great footmen in knee-breeches who sleep in the big arm-chairs, made drowsy by the heavy warmth of the hot-air stove. She thought of the long *salons* fitted up with ancient silk, of the delicate furniture carrying priceless curiosities, and of the coquettish perfumed boudoirs made for talks at five o'clock with intimate friends, with men famous and sought after, whom all women envy and whose attention they all desire.

When she sat down to dinner, before the round table covered with a table-cloth three days old, opposite her husband, who uncovered the soup-tureen and declared with an enchanted air, "Ah, the good *pot-au-feu!* I don't know anything better than that," she thought of dainty dinners, of shining silverware, of tapestry which peopled the walls with ancient personages and with strange birds flying in the midst of a fairy forest; and she thought of delicious dishes served on marvellous plates, and of the whispered gallantries which you listen to with a sphinx-like smile, while you are eating the pink flesh of a trout or the wings of a quail.

She had no dresses, no jewels, nothing. And she loved nothing but that; she felt made for that. She would so have liked to please, to be envied, to be charming, to be sought after.

She had a friend, a former school-mate at the convent, who was rich, and whom she did not like to go and see any more, because she suffered so much when she came back.

But, one evening, her husband returned

home with a triumphant air, and holding a large envelope in his hand.

"There," said he, "here is something for you."

She tore the paper sharply, and drew out a printed card which bore these words:

"The Minister of Public Instruction and Mme. Georges Ramponneau request the honor of M. and Mme. Loisel's company at the palace of the Ministry on Monday evening, January 18th."

Instead of being delighted, as her husband hoped, she threw the invitation on the table with disdain, murmuring:

"What do you want me to do with that?"

"But, my dear, I thought you would be glad. You never go out, and this is such a fine opportunity. I had awful trouble to get it. Every one wants to go; it is very select, and they are not giving many invitations to clerks. The whole official world will be there."

She looked at him with an irritated eye, and she said, impatiently:

"And what do you want me to put on my back?"

He had not thought of that; he stammered:

"Why, the dress you go to the theatre in. It looks very well, to me."

He stopped, distracted, seeing that his wife was crying. Two great tears descended slowly from the corners of her eyes towards the corners of her mouth. He stuttered:

"What's the matter? What's the matter?"

But, by a violent effort, she had conquered her grief, and she replied, with a calm voice, while she wiped her wet cheeks:

"Nothing. Only I have no dress, and therefore I can't go to this ball. Give your card to some colleague whose wife is better equipped than I."

He was in despair. He resumed:

"Come, let us see, Mathilde. How much would it cost, a suitable dress, which you could use on other occasions, something very simple?"

She reflected several seconds, making her calculations and wondering also what sum she could ask without drawing on herself an immediate refusal and a frightened exclamation from the economical clerk.

Finally, she replied, hesitatingly:

"I don't know exactly, but I think I could manage it with four hundred francs."

He had grown a little pale, because he was laying aside just that amount to buy a gun and treat himself to a little shooting next summer on the plain of Nanterre, with several friends who went to shoot larks down there, of a Sunday.

But he said:

"All right. I will give you four hundred francs. And try to have a pretty dress."

The day of the ball drew near, and Mme. Loisel seemed sad, uneasy, anxious. Her dress was ready, however. Her husband said to her one evening:

"What is the matter? Come, you've been so queer these last three days."

And she answered:

"It annoys me not to have a single jewel, not a single stone, nothing to put on. I

THE NECKLACE. 59

shall look like distress. I should almost rather not go at all."

He resumed:

"You might wear natural flowers. It's very stylish at this time of the year. For ten francs you can get two or three magnificent roses."

She was not convinced.

"No; there's nothing more humiliating than to look poor among other women who are rich."

But her husband cried:

"How stupid you are! Go look up your friend Mme. Forestier, and ask her to lend you some jewels. You're quite thick enough with her to do that."

She uttered a cry of joy:

"It's true. I never thought of it."

The next day she went to her friend and told of her distress.

Mme. Forestier went to a wardrobe with a glass door, took out a large jewel-box, brought it back, opened it, and said to Mme. Loisel:

"Choose, my dear."

She saw first of all some bracelets, then a pearl necklace, then a Venetian cross, gold and precious stones of admirable workmanship. She tried on the ornaments before the glass, hesitated, could not make up her mind to part with them, to give them back. She kept asking:

"Haven't you any more?"

"Why, yes. Look. I don't know what you like."

All of a sudden she discovered, in a black satin box, a superb necklace of diamonds; and her heart began to beat with an immoderate desire. Her hands trembled as she took it. She fastened it around her throat, outside her high-necked dress, and remained lost in ecstasy at the sight of herself.

Then she asked, hesitating, filled with anguish:

"Can you lend me that, only that?"

"Why, yes, certainly."

She sprang upon the neck of her friend, kissed her passionately, then fled with her treasure.

The day of the ball arrived. Mme. Loisel made a great success. She was prettier than them all, elegant, gracious, smiling, and crazy with joy. All the men looked at her, asked her name, endeavored to be introduced. All the attachés of the Cabinet wanted to waltz with her. She was remarked by the minister himself.

She danced with intoxication, with passion, made drunk by pleasure, forgetting all, in the triumph of her beauty, in the glory of her success, in a sort of cloud of happiness composed of all this homage, of all this admiration, of all these awakened desires, and of that sense of complete victory which is so sweet to woman's heart.

She went away about four o'clock in the morning. Her husband had been sleeping since midnight, in a little deserted anteroom, with three other gentlemen whose wives were having a very good time.

He threw over her shoulders the wraps which he had brought, modest wraps of common life, whose poverty contrasted with the elegance of the ball dress. She felt this and wanted to escape so as not to be remarked by the other women, who were enveloping themselves in costly furs.

Loisel held her back.

"Wait a bit. You will catch cold outside. I will go and call a cab."

But she did not listen to him, and rapidly descended the stairs. When they were in the street they did not find a carriage; and they began to look for one, shouting after the cabmen whom they saw passing by at a distance.

They went down towards the Seine, in despair, shivering with cold. At last they found on the quay one of those ancient noctambulant coupés which, exactly as if they were ashamed to show their misery during the day, are never seen round Paris until after nightfall.

It took them to their door in the Rue des Martyrs, and once more, sadly, they climbed up homeward. All was ended, for her. And as to him, he reflected that he must be at the Ministry at ten o'clock.

She removed the wraps, which covered her shoulders, before the glass, so as once more to see herself in all her glory. But suddenly she uttered a cry. She had no longer the necklace around her neck!

Her husband, already half-undressed, demanded:

"What is the matter with you?"

She turned madly towards him:

"I have—I have—I've lost Mme. Forestier's necklace."

He stood up, distracted.

"What!—how?—Impossible!"

And they looked in the folds of her dress, in the folds of her cloak, in her pockets, everywhere. They did not find it.

He asked:

"You're sure you had it on when you left the ball?"

"Yes, I felt it in the vestibule of the palace."

"But if you had lost it in the street we should have heard it fall. It must be in the cab."

"Yes. Probably. Did you take his number?"

"No. And you, didn't you notice it?"

"No."

They looked, thunderstruck, at one another. At last Loisel put on his clothes.

"I shall go back on foot," said he, "over

the whole route which we have taken, to see if I can't find it."

And he went out. She sat waiting on a chair in her ball dress, without strength to go to bed, overwhelmed, without fire, without a thought.

Her husband came back about seven o'clock. He had found nothing.

He went to Police Headquarters, to the newspaper offices, to offer a reward; he went to the cab companies—everywhere, in fact, whither he was urged by the least suspicion of hope.

She waited all day, in the same condition of mad fear before this terrible calamity.

Loisel returned at night with a hollow, pale face; he had discovered nothing.

"You must write to your friend," said he, "that you have broken the clasp of her necklace and that you are having it mended. That will give us time to turn round."

She wrote at his dictation.

At the end of a week they had lost all hope.

And Loisel, who had aged five years, declared:

"We must consider how to replace that ornament."

The next day they took the box which had contained it, and they went to the jeweller whose name was found within. He consulted his books.

"It was not I, madame, who sold that necklace; I must simply have furnished the case."

Then they went from jeweller to jeweller, searching for a necklace like the other, consulting their memories, sick both of them with chagrin and with anguish.

They found, in a shop at the Palais Royal, a string of diamonds which seemed to them exactly like the one they looked for. It was worth forty thousand francs. They could have it for thirty-six.

So they begged the jeweller not to sell it for three days yet. And they made a bargain that he should buy it back for thirty-four thousand francs, in case they found the other one before the end of February.

Loisel possessed eighteen thousand francs which his father had left him. He would borrow the rest.

He did borrow, asking a thousand francs of one, five hundred of another, five louis here, three louis there. He gave notes, took up ruinous obligations, dealt with usurers, and all the race of lenders. He compromised all the rest of his life, risked his signature without even knowing if he could meet it; and, frightened by the pains yet to come, by the black misery which was about to fall upon him, by the prospect of all the physical privations and of all the moral tortures which he was to suffer, he went to get the new necklace, putting down upon the merchant's counter thirty-six thousand francs.

When Mme. Loisel took back the necklace, Mme. Forestier said to her, with a chilly manner:

"You should have returned it sooner, I might have needed it."

She did not open the case, as her friend had so much feared. If she had detected the substitution, what would she have thought, what would she have said? Would she not have taken Mme. Loisel for a thief?

Mme. Loisel now knew the horrible existence of the needy. She took her part, moreover, all on a sudden, with heroism. That dreadful debt must be paid. She would pay it. They dismissed their servant; they changed their lodgings; they rented a garret under the roof.

She came to know what heavy housework meant and the odious cares of the kitchen. She washed the dishes, using her rosy nails on the greasy pots and pans. She washed the dirty linen, the shirts, and the dish-cloths, which she dried upon a line; she carried the slops down to the street every morning, and carried up the water, stopping for breath at every landing. And, dressed like a woman of the people, she went to the fruiterer, the grocer, the butcher, her basket on her arm, bargaining, insulted, defending her miserable money sou by sou.

Each month they had to meet some notes, renew others, obtain more time.

Her husband worked in the evening making a fair copy of some tradesman's accounts, and late at night he often copied manuscript for five sous a page.

And this life lasted ten years.

At the end of ten years they had paid everything, everything, with the rates of usury, and the accumulations of the compound interest.

Mme. Loisel looked old now. She had become the woman of impoverished households—strong and hard and rough. With frowsy hair, skirts askew, and red hands, she talked loud while washing the floor with great swishes of water. But sometimes, when her husband was at the office, she sat down near the window, and she thought of that gay evening of long ago, of that ball where she had been so beautiful and so fêted.

What would have happened if she had not lost that necklace? Who knows? who knows? How life is strange and changeful! How little a thing is needed for us to be lost or to be saved!

But, one Sunday, having gone to take a walk in the Champs Élysées to refresh herself from the labors of the week, she suddenly perceived a woman who was leading a child. It was Mme. Forestier, still young, still beautiful, still charming.

Mme. Loisel felt moved. Was she going to speak to her? Yes, certainly. And now that she had paid, she was going to tell her all about it. Why not?

She went up.

"Good-day, Jeanne."

The other, astonished to be familiarly addressed by this plain good-wife, did not recognize her at all, and stammered:

"But—madame!—I do not know— You must have mistaken."

"No. I am Mathilde Loisel."

Her friend uttered a cry.

"Oh, my poor Mathilde! How you are changed!"

"Yes, I have had days hard enough, since I have seen you, days wretched enough— and that because of you!"

"Of me! How so?"

"Do you remember that diamond necklace which you lent me to wear at the ministerial ball?"

"Yes. Well?"

"Well, I lost it."

"What do you mean? You brought it back."

"I brought you back another just like it. And for this we have been ten years paying. You can understand that it was not easy for us, us who had nothing. At last it is ended, and I am very glad."

Mme. Forestier had stopped.

"You say that you bought a necklace of diamonds to replace mine?"

"Yes. You never noticed it, then! They were very like."

And she smiled with a joy which was proud and naïve at once.

Mme. Forestier, strongly moved, took her two hands.

"Oh, my poor Mathilde! Why, my necklace was paste. It was worth at most five hundred francs!"

V.

THE PIECE OF STRING.

THE PIECE OF STRING.

It was market-day, and over all the roads round Goderville the peasants and their wives were coming towards the town. The men walked easily, lurching the whole body forward at every step. Their long legs were twisted and deformed by the slow, painful labors of the country:—by bending over to plough, which is what also makes their left shoulders too high and their figures crooked; and by reaping corn, which obliges them for steadiness' sake to spread their knees too wide. Their starched blue blouses, shining as though varnished, ornamented at collar and cuffs with little patterns of white stitch-work, and blown up big around their bony bodies, seemed exactly like balloons about to soar, but putting forth a head, two arms, and two feet.

Some of these fellows dragged a cow or a calf at the end of a rope. And just behind the animal, beating it over the back with a leaf-covered branch to hasten its pace, went their wives, carrying large baskets from which came forth the heads of chickens or the heads of ducks. These women walked with steps far shorter and quicker than the men; their figures, withered and upright, were adorned with scanty little shawls pinned over their flat bosoms; and they enveloped their heads each in a white cloth, close fastened round the hair and surmounted by a cap.

Now a char-à-banc passed by, drawn by a jerky-paced nag. It shook up strangely the two men on the seat. And the woman at the bottom of the cart held fast to its sides to lessen the hard joltings.

In the market-place at Goderville was a great crowd, a mingled multitude of men and beasts. The horns of cattle, the high and long-napped hats of wealthy peasants, the head-dresses of the women, came to the surface of that sea. And voices clamorous, sharp, shrill, made a continuous and savage din. Above it a huge burst of laughter from the sturdy lungs of a merry yokel would sometimes sound, and sometimes a long bellow from a cow tied fast to the wall of a house.

It all smelled of the stable, of milk, of hay, and of perspiration, giving off that half-human, half-animal odor which is peculiar to the men of the fields.

Maître Hauchecorne, of Bréauté, had just arrived at Goderville, and was taking his way towards the square, when he perceived on the ground a little piece of string. Maître Hauchecorne, economical, like all true Normans, reflected that everything was worth picking up which could be of any use; and he stooped down—but painfully, because he suffered from rheumatism. He took the bit of thin cord from the ground, and was carefully preparing to roll it up when he saw Maître Malandain, the harness-maker, on his door-step, looking at him. They had once had a quarrel about a halter, and they had remained angry, bearing malice on both sides. Maître Hauchecorne was overcome with a sort of shame at being seen by his enemy looking in the dirt so for a bit of string. He quickly hid his find beneath his blouse; then in the pocket of his breeches; then pretended to be still looking for something on the ground which he did not discover; and at last went off towards the market-place, with his head bent forward, and a body almost doubled in two by rheumatic pains.

He lost himself immediately in the crowd, which was clamorous, slow, and agitated by interminable bargains. The peasants examined the cows, went off, came back, always in great perplexity and fear of being cheated, never quite daring to decide, spying at the eye of the seller, trying ceaselessly to discover the tricks of the man and the defect in the beast.

The women, having placed their great baskets at their feet, had pulled out the poultry, which lay upon the ground, tied by the legs, with eyes scared, with combs scarlet.

They listened to propositions, maintaining their prices, with a dry manner, with an impassible face; or, suddenly, perhaps, deciding to take the lower price which was offered, they cried out to the customer, who was departing slowly:

"All right, I'll let you have them, Mâit' Anthime."

Then, little by little, the square became empty, and when the *Angelus* struck midday those who lived at a distance poured into the inns.

At Jourdain's the great room was filled with eaters, just as the vast court was filled with vehicles of every sort—wagons, gigs, char-à-bancs, tilburys, tilt-carts which have no name, yellow with mud, misshapen, pieced together, raising their shafts to heaven like two arms, or it may be with their nose in the dirt and their rear in the air.

Just opposite to where the diners were at table the huge fireplace, full of clear flame, threw a lively heat on the backs of those who sat along the right. Three spits were turning, loaded with chickens, with pigeons, and with joints of mutton; and a delectable odor of roast meat, and of gravy gushing over crisp brown skin, took wing from the hearth, kindled merriment, caused mouths to water.

All the aristocracy of the plough were eating there, at Maît' Jourdain's, the innkeeper's, a dealer in horses also, and a sharp fellow who had made a pretty penny in his day.

The dishes were passed round, were emptied, with jugs of yellow cider. Every one told of his affairs, of his purchases and his sales. They asked news about the crops. The weather was good for green stuffs, but a little wet for wheat.

All of a sudden the drum rolled in the court before the house. Every one, except some of the most indifferent, was on his feet at once, and ran to the door, to the windows, with his mouth still full and his napkin in his hand.

When the public crier had finished his tattoo he called forth in a jerky voice, making his pauses out of time:

" Be it known to the inhabitants of Goderville, and in general to all—persons present at the market, that there has been lost this morning, on the Beuzeville road, between—nine and ten o'clock, a pocket-book of black leather, containing five hundred francs and business papers. You are requested to return it—to the mayor's office, at once, or to Maître Fortuné Houlbrèque, of Manneville. There will be twenty francs reward."

Then the man departed. They heard once more at a distance the dull beatings on the drum and the faint voice of the crier.

Then they began to talk of this event, reckoning up the chances which Maître Houlbrèque had of finding or of not finding his pocket-book again.

And the meal went on.

They were finishing their coffee when the corporal of gendarmes appeared on the threshold.

He asked:

"Is Maître Hauchecorne, of Bréauté, here?"

Maître Hauchecorne, seated at the other end of the table, answered:

"Here I am."

And the corporal resumed:

"Maître Hauchecorne, will you have the kindness to come with me to the mayor's office? M. le Maire would like to speak to you."

The peasant, surprised and uneasy, gulped down his little glass of cognac, got up, and, even worse bent over than in the morning, since the first steps after a rest were always particularly difficult, started off, repeating:

"Here I am, here I am."

And he followed the corporal.

The mayor was waiting for him, seated in an arm-chair. He was the notary of the place, a tall, grave man of pompous speech.

"Maître Hauchecorne," said he, "this morning, on the Beuzeville road, you were seen to pick up the pocket-book lost by Maître Houlbrèque, of Manneville."

The countryman, speechless, regarded the mayor, frightened already by this suspicion which rested on him he knew not why.

"I, I picked up that pocket-book?"

"Yes, you."

"I swear I didn't even know nothing about it at all."

"You were seen."

"They saw me, me? Who is that who saw me?"

"M. Malandain, the harness-maker."

Then the old man remembered, understood, and, reddening with anger:

"Ah! he saw me, did he, the rascal? He saw me picking up this string here, M'sieu' le Maire."

And, fumbling at the bottom of his pocket, he pulled out of it the little end of string.

But the mayor incredulously shook his head:

"You will not make me believe, Maître Hauchecorne, that M. Malandain, who is a man worthy of credit, has mistaken this string for a pocket-book."

The peasant, furious, raised his hand and spit as if to attest his good faith, repeating:

"For all that, it is the truth of the good God, the blessed truth, M'sieu' le Maire. There! on my soul and my salvation I repeat it."

The mayor continued:

"After having picked up the thing in question, you even looked for some time in the mud to see if a piece of money had not dropped out of it."

The good man was suffocated with indignation and with fear:

"If they can say!—if they can say .... such lies as that to slander an honest man! If they can say!—"

He might protest, he was not believed.

He was confronted with M. Malandain, who repeated and sustained his testimony. They abused one another for an hour. At his own request Maître Hauchecorne was searched. Nothing was found upon him.

At last, the mayor, much perplexed, sent him away, warning him that he would inform the public prosecutor, and ask for orders.

The news had spread. When he left the mayor's office, the old man was surrounded, interrogated with a curiosity which was serious or mocking as the case might be, but into which no indignation entered. And he began to tell the story of the string. They did not believe him. They laughed.

He passed on, button-holed by every one, himself button-holing his acquaintances, beginning over and over again his tale and his protestations, showing his pockets turned inside out to prove that he had nothing.

They said to him:

"You old rogue, *va!*"

And he grew angry, exasperated, feverish, in despair at not being believed, and always telling his story.

The night came. It was time to go home. He set out with three of his neighbors, to whom he pointed out the place where he had picked up the end of string; and all the way he talked of his adventure.

That evening he made the round in the village of Bréauté, so as to tell every one. He met only unbelievers.

He was ill of it all night long.

The next day, about one in the afternoon, Marius Paumelle, a farm hand of Maître Breton, the market-gardener at Ymauville, returned the pocket-book and its contents to Maître Houlbrèque, of Manneville.

This man said, indeed, that he had found it on the road; but not knowing how to read, he had carried it home and given it to his master.

The news spread to the environs. Maître Hauchecorne was informed. He put himself at once upon the go, and began to relate-

his story as completed by the *dénouement*. He triumphed.

"What grieved me," said he, "was not the thing itself, do you understand; but it was the lies. There's nothing does you so much harm as being in disgrace for lying."

All day he talked of his adventure, he told it on the roads to the people who passed; at the cabaret to the people who drank; and the next Sunday, when they came out of church. He even stopped strangers to tell them about it. He was easy, now, and yet something worried him without his knowing exactly what it was. People had a joking manner while they listened. They did not seem convinced. He seemed to feel their tittle-tattle behind his back.

On Tuesday of the next week he went to market at Goderville, prompted entirely by the need of telling his story.

Malandain, standing on his door-step, began to laugh as he saw him pass. Why?

He accosted a farmer of Criquetot, who did not let him finish, and, giving him a punch in the pit of his stomach, cried in his face:

"Oh you great rogue, *va !*" Then turned his heel upon him.

Maître Hauchecorne remained speechless, and grew more and more uneasy. Why had they called him "great rogue?"

When seated at table in Jourdain's tavern he began again to explain the whole affair.

A horse-dealer of Montivilliers shouted at him:

"Get out, get out you old scamp; I know all about your string!"

Hauchecorne stammered:

"But since they found it again, the pocket-book!"

But the other continued:

"Hold your tongue, daddy; there's one who finds it and there's another who returns it. And no one the wiser."

The peasant was choked. He understood at last. They accused him of having had the pocket-book brought back by an accomplice, by a confederate.

He tried to protest. The whole table began to laugh.

He could not finish his dinner, and went away amid a chorus of jeers.

He went home, ashamed and indignant, choked with rage, with confusion, the more cast-down since from his Norman cunning, he was, perhaps, capable of having done what they accused him of, and even of boasting of it as a good trick. His innocence dimly seemed to him impossible to prove, his craftiness being so well known. And he felt himself struck to the heart by the injustice of the suspicion.

Then he began anew to tell of his adventure, lengthening his recital every day, each time adding new proofs, more energetic protestations, and more solemn oaths which he thought of, which he prepared in his hours of solitude, his mind being entirely occupied by the story of the string. The more complicated his defence, the more artful his arguments, the less he was believed.

"Those are liars' proofs," they said behind his back.

He felt this; it preyed upon his heart. He exhausted himself in useless efforts.

He was visibly wasting away.

The jokers now made him tell the story of "The Piece of String" to amuse them.

just as you make a soldier who has been on a campaign tell his story of the battle. His mind, struck at the root, grew weak.

About the end of December he took to his bed.

He died early in January, and, in the delirium of the death-agony, he protested his innocence, repeating:

"A little bit of string — a little bit of string — see, here it is, M'sieu' le Maire."

VI.

LA MÈRE SAUVAGE.

LA MÈRE SAUVAGE.

I HAD not been at Virelogne for fifteen years. I went back there in the autumn, to shoot with my friend Serval, who had at last rebuilt his château, which had been destroyed by the Prussians.

I loved that district very much. It is one of those corners of the world which have a sensuous charm for the eyes. You love it with a bodily love. We, whom the country seduces, we keep tender memories for certain springs, for certain woods, for certain pools, for certain hills, seen very often, and which have stirred us like joyful events. Sometimes our thoughts turn back towards a corner in a forest, or the end of a bank, or an orchard powdered with flowers, seen but a single time, on some gay day; yet remaining in our hearts like the images of certain women met in the street on a spring morning, with bright transparent dresses; and leaving in soul and body an unappeased desire which is not to be forgotten, a feeling that you have just rubbed elbows with happiness.

At Virelogne I loved the whole countryside, dotted with little woods, and crossed by brooks which flashed in the sun and looked like veins, carrying blood to the earth. You fished in them for crawfish, trout, and eels! Divine happiness! You could bathe in places, and you often found snipe among the high grass which grew along the borders of these slender watercourses.

I was walking, lightly as a goat, watching my two dogs ranging before me. Serval, a hundred metres to my right, was beating a field of lucern. I turned the thicket which forms the boundary of the wood of Sandres, and I saw a cottage in ruins.

All of a sudden, I remembered it as I had seen it the last time, in 1869, neat, covered with vines, with chickens before the door.

What sadder than a dead house, with its skeleton standing upright, bare and sinister?

I also remembered that in it, one very tiring day, the good woman had given me a glass of wine to drink, and that Serval had then told me the history of its inhabitants. The father, an old poacher, had been killed by the gendarmes. The son, whom I had once seen, was a tall, dry fellow who also passed for a ferocious destroyer of game. People called them "les Sauvage."

Was that a name or a nickname?

I hailed Serval. He came up with his long strides like a crane.

I asked him:

"What's become of those people?"

And he told me this story:

When war was declared, the son Sauvage, who was then thirty-three years old, enlisted, leaving his mother alone in the house. People did not pity the old woman very much, because she had money; they knew it.

But she remained quite alone in that isolated dwelling so far from the village, on the edge of the wood. She was not afraid, however, being of the same strain as her menfolk; a hardy old woman, tall and thin, who laughed seldom, and with whom one never jested. The women of the fields laugh but little in any case; that is men's business, that! But they themselves have sad and narrowed hearts, leading a melancholy, gloomy life. The peasants learn a little boisterous merriment at the tavern, but their helpmates remain grave, with countenances which are always severe. The muscles of their faces have never learned the movements of the laugh.

La Mère Sauvage continued her ordinary existence in her cottage, which was soon covered by the snows. She came to the village once a week, to get bread and a little meat; then she returned into her house. As there was talk of wolves, she went out with a gun upon her back—her son's gun, rusty, and with the butt worn by the rubbing of the hand; and she was strange to see, the tall "Sauvage," a little bent, going with slow strides over the snow, the muzzle of the piece extending beyond the black head-dress, which pressed close to her head and imprisoned her white hair, which no one had ever seen.

One day a Prussian force arrived. It was billeted upon the inhabitants, according to the property and resources of each. Four were allotted to the old woman, who was known to be rich.

They were four great boys with blond skin, with blond beards, with blue eyes, who had remained stout notwithstanding the fatigues which they had endured already, and who also, though in a conquered country, had remained kind and gentle. Alone with this aged woman, they showed themselves full of consideration, sparing her, as much as they could, all expenses and fatigue. They would be seen, all four of them, making their toilet round the well, of a morning, in their shirt-sleeves, splashing with great swishes of water, under the crude daylight of the snowy weather, their pink-white Northman's flesh, while La Mère Sauvage went and came, making ready the soup. Then they would be seen cleaning the kitchen, rubbing the tiles, splitting wood, peeling potatoes, doing up all the house-work, like four good sons about their mother.

But the old woman thought always of her own, so tall and thin, with his hooked nose and his brown eyes and his heavy mustache which made a roll of black hairs upon his lip. She asked each day of each of the soldiers who were installed beside her hearth:

"Do you know where the French Marching Regiment No. 23 was sent? My boy is in it."

They answered, "No, not know, not know at all." And, understanding her pain and her uneasiness (they, who had mothers too, there at home), they rendered her a thousand little services. She loved them well, moreover, her four enemies, since the peasantry feels no patriotic hatred; that belongs to the upper class alone. The humble, those who pay the most, because they are poor, and because every new burden crushes them down; those who are killed in masses, who make the true cannon's-meat, because they are so many; those, in fine, who suffer most cruelly the atrocious miseries of war, because they are the feeblest, and offer least resistance—they hardly understand at all those bellicose ardors, that excitable sense of honor, or those pretended political combinations which in six months exhaust two nations, the conqueror with the conquered.

They said on the country-side, in speaking of the Germans of La Mère Sauvage:

"There are four who have found a soft place."

Now, one morning, when the old woman was alone in the house, she perceived far off on the plain a man coming towards her dwelling. Soon she recognized him; it was the postman charged to distribute the letters. He gave her a folded paper, and she drew out of her case the spectacles which she used for sewing; then she read:

"MADAME SAUVAGE,—The present letter is to tell you sad news. Your boy Victor was killed yesterday by a shell which near cut him in two. I was just by, seeing that we stood next each other in the company, and he would talk to me about you to let you know on the same day if anything happened to him.

"I took his watch, which was in his pocket, to bring it back to you when the war is done.

"I salute you very friendly.

"Césaire Rivot,
"Soldier of the 2d class, March. Reg. No. 23."

The letter was dated three weeks back.

She did not cry at all. She remained motionless, so seized and stupefied that she did not even suffer as yet. She thought: "V'la Victor who is killed now." Then little by little the tears mounted to her eyes, and the sorrow caught her heart. The ideas came to her, one by one, dreadful, torturing. She would never kiss him again, her child, her big boy, never again! The gendarmes had killed the father, the Prussians had killed the son. He had been cut in two by a cannon-ball. She seemed to see the thing, the horrible thing: the head falling, the eyes open, while he chewed the corner of his big mustache as he always did in moments of anger.

What had they done with his body afterwards? If they had only let her have her boy back as they had given her back her husband—with the bullet in the middle of his forehead!

But she heard a noise of voices. It was the Prussians returning from the village. She hid her letter very quickly in her pocket, and she received them quietly, with her ordinary face, having had time to wipe her eyes.

They were laughing, all four, delighted, since they brought with them a fine rabbit—stolen, doubtless—and they made signs to the old woman that there was to be something good to eat.

She set herself to work at once to prepare breakfast; but when it came to killing the rabbit, her heart failed her. And yet it was not the first. One of the soldiers struck it down with a blow of his fist behind the ears.

The beast once dead, she separated the red body from the skin; but the sight of the blood which she was touching, and which covered her hands, of the warm blood which she felt cooling and coagulating, made her tremble from head to foot; and she kept seeing her big boy cut in two, and quite red also, like this still palpitating animal.

She set herself at table with the Prussians, but she could not eat, not even a mouthful. They devoured the rabbit without troubling themselves about her. She looked at them askance, without speaking, ripening a thought, and with a face so impassible that they perceived nothing.

All of a sudden, she said: "I don't even know your names, and here's a whole month that we've been together." They understood, not without difficulty, what she wanted, and told their names. That was not sufficient; she had them written for her on a paper, with the addresses of their families, and, resting her spectacles on her great nose, she considered that strange handwriting, then folded the sheet and put it in her pocket, on top of the letter which told her of the death of her son.

When the meal was ended, she said to the men:

"I am going to work for you."

And she began to carry up hay into the loft where they slept.

They were astonished at her taking all this trouble; she explained to them that thus they would not be so cold; and they helped her. They heaped the trusses of hay as high as the straw roof; and in that manner they made a sort of great chamber with four walls of fodder, warm and perfumed, where they should sleep splendidly.

At dinner, one of them was worried to see that La Mère Sauvage still ate nothing. She told him that she had the cramps. Then she kindled a good fire to warm herself up, and the four Germans mounted to their lodging-place by the ladder which served them every night for this purpose.

As soon as they closed the trap, the old woman removed the ladder, then opened the outside door noiselessly, and went back to look for more bundles of straw, with which she filled her kitchen. She went barefoot in the snow, so softly that no sound was heard. From time to time she listened to the sonorous and unequal snorings of the four soldiers who were fast asleep.

When she judged her preparations to be sufficient, she threw one of the bundles into the fireplace, and when it was alight she scattered it over all the others. Then she went outside again and looked.

In a few seconds the whole interior of the cottage was illumined with a violent brightness and became a dreadful brasier, a gigantic fiery furnace, whose brilliance spouted out of the narrow window and threw a glittering beam upon the snòw.

Then a great cry issued from the summit of the house; it was a clamor of human shriekings, heart-rending calls of anguish and of fear. At last, the trap having fallen in, a whirlwind of fire shot up into the loft, pierced the straw roof, rose to the sky like the immense flame of a torch; and all the cottage flared.

Nothing more was heard therein but the crackling of the fire, the crackling sound of the walls, the falling of the rafters. All of a sudden the roof fell in, and the burning carcass of the dwelling hurled a great plume of sparks into the air, amid a cloud of smoke.

The country, all white, lit up by the fire, shone like a cloth of silver tinted with red.

A bell, far off, began to toll.

The old "Sauvage" remained standing before her ruined dwelling, armed with her gun, her son's gun, for fear lest one of those men might escape.

When she saw that it was ended, she threw her weapon into the brasier. A loud report rang back.

People were coming, the peasants, the Prussians.

They found the woman seated on the trunk of a tree, calm and satisfied.

A German officer, who spoke French like a son of France, demanded of her:

"Where are your soldiers?"

She extended her thin arm towards the red heap of fire which was gradually going out, and she answered with a strong voice:

"There!"

They crowded round her. The Prussian asked:

"How did it take fire?"

She said:

"It was I who set it on fire."

They did not believe her, they thought that the sudden disaster had made her crazy. So, while all pressed round and listened, she told the thing from one end to the other, from the arrival of the letter to the last cry of the men who were burned with her house. She did not forget a detail of all which she had felt, nor of all which she had done.

When she had finished, she drew two pieces of paper from her pocket, and, to distinguish them by the last glimmers of the fire, she again adjusted her spectacles; then she said, showing one: "That, that is the death of Victor." Showing the other, she added, indicating the red ruins with a bend of the head: "That, that is their names, so that you can write home." She calmly held the white sheet out to the officer, who held her by the shoulders, and she continued:

"You must write how it happened, and you must say to their mothers that it was I who did that, Victoire Simon, la Sauvage! Do not forget."

The officer shouted some orders in German. They seized her, they threw her against the walls of her house, still hot. Then twelve men drew quickly up before her, at twenty paces. She did not move. She had understood; she waited.

An order rang out, followed instantly by a long report. A belated shot went off by itself, after the others.

The old woman did not fall. She sank as though they had mowed off her legs.

The Prussian officer approached. She was almost cut in two, and in her withered hand she held her letter bathed with blood.

My friend Serval added:

"It was by way of reprisal that the Germans destroyed the château of the district, which belonged to me."

As for me, I thought of the mothers of those four gentle fellows burned in that house; and of the atrocious heroism of that other mother shot against the wall.

And I picked up a little stone, still blackened by the flames.

VII.
MOONLIGHT.

MOONLIGHT.

The Abbé Marignan, as soldier of the Church, bore his fighting title well. He was a tall, thin priest, very fanatical, of an ecstatic but upright soul. All his beliefs were fixed, without ever a wavering. He thought that he understood God thoroughly, that he penetrated His designs, His wishes, His intentions.

When he promenaded with great strides in the garden walk of his little country parsonage, sometimes a question rose in his mind: "Why did God make that?" And in fancy taking the place of God, he searched obstinately, and nearly always he found the reason. It is not he who would have murmured in a transport of pious humility,

"O Lord, thy ways are past finding out!" He said to himself, "I am the servant of God; I ought to know the reason of what He does, or to divine it if I do not."

Everything in nature seemed to him created with an absolute and admirable logic. The "wherefore" and the "because" were always balanced. The dawns were made to render glad your waking, the days to ripen the harvests, the rains to water them, the evenings to prepare for sleeping, and the nights dark for sleep.

The four seasons corresponded perfectly to all the needs of agriculture; and to him the suspicion could never have come that nature has no intentions, and that all which lives has bent itself, on the contrary, to the hard conditions of different periods, of climates, and of matter.

Only he did hate women; he hated them unconscionably, and he despised them by instinct. He often repeated the words of Christ, "Woman, what have I to do with thee?" and he added, "One would almost say that God himself was ill-pleased with that particular work of his hands." Woman was indeed for him the "child twelve times unclean" of whom the poet speaks. She was the temptress who had ensnared the first man, and who still continued her work of damnation; she was the being who is feeble, dangerous, mysteriously troubling. And even more than her body of perdition, he hated her loving soul.

He had often felt women's tenderness attach itself to him, and though he knew himself to be unassailable, he grew exasperated at that need of loving which quivered always in their hearts.

God, to his mind, had only created woman to tempt man and to prove him. You should not approach her without those precautions for defence which you would take, and those fears which you would cherish, near a trap. She was, indeed, just like a trap, with her arms extended and her lips open towards a man.

He had indulgence only for nuns, rendered harmless by their vow; but he treated them harshly notwithstanding, because, ever living at the bottom of their chained-up hearts, of their chastened hearts, he perceived that eternal tenderness which constantly went out to him, although he was a priest.

He was conscious of it in their looks more moist with piety than the looks of monks, in their ecstasies, in their transports of love towards the Christ, which angered him because it was women's love; and he was also conscious of it, of that accursed tenderness, in their very docility, in the softness of their voices when they spoke to him, in their lowered eyes, and in the meekness of their tears when he reproved them roughly.

And he shook his cassock on issuing from the doors of the convent, and he went off with long strides, as though he had fled before some danger.

He had a niece who lived with her mother in a little house near by. He was bent on making her a sister of charity.

She was pretty, and hare-brained, and a great tease. When the abbé sermonized, she laughed; when he was angry at her, she kissed him vehemently, pressing him to her heart, while he would seek involuntarily to free himself from this embrace, which, notwithstanding, made him taste a certain sweet joy, awaking deep within him that sensation of fatherhood which slumbers in every man.

Often he talked to her of God, of his God, walking beside her along the foot-paths through the fields. She hardly listened, and looked at the sky, the grass, the flowers with a joy of living which could be seen in her eyes. Sometimes she rushed forward to catch some flying creature, and bringing it back, would cry: "Look, my uncle, how pretty it is; I should like to kiss it." And this necessity to "kiss flies," or lilac berries, worried, irritated, and revolted the priest, who saw, even in that, the ineradicable tenderness which ever springs at the hearts of women.

And now one day the sacristan's wife, who kept house for the Abbé Marignan, told him, very cautiously, that his niece had a lover!

He experienced a dreadful emotion, and he stood choked, with the soap all over his face, being in the act of shaving.

When he found himself able to think and

speak once more, he cried: "It is not true; you are lying, Mélanie!"

But the peasant woman put her hand on her heart: "May our Lord judge me if I am lying, Monsieur le Curé. I tell you she goes to him every evening as soon as your sister is in bed. They meet each other beside the river. You have only to go there between ten o'clock and midnight, and see for yourself."

He ceased scratching his chin, and he commenced to walk the room violently, as he always did in his hours of gravest thought. When he tried to begin his shaving again, he cut himself three times from nose to ear.

All day long, he remained silent, swollen with anger and with rage. To his priestly zeal against the mighty power of love was added the moral indignation of a father, of a teacher, of a keeper of souls, who has been deceived, robbed, played with by a child. He had that egotistical choking sensation such as parents feel when their daughter anounces that she has chosen a husband without them and in spite of their advice.

After his dinner, he tried to read a little, but he could not bring himself so far; and he grew angrier and angrier. When it struck ten, he took his cane, a formidable oaken club which he always carried when he had to go out at night to visit the sick. And he smilingly regarded the enormous cudgel, holding it in his solid, countryman's fist and cutting threatening circles with it in the air. Then, suddenly he raised it, and grinding his teeth, he brought it down upon a chair, the back of which, split in two, fell heavily to the ground.

He opened his door to go out; but he stopped upon the threshold, surprised by such a splendor of moonlight as you seldom see.

And since he was endowed with an exalted spirit, such a spirit as must have belonged to those dreamer-poets, the Fathers of the Church, he felt himself suddenly distracted, moved by the grand and serene beauty of the pale-faced night.

In his little garden, quite bathed with the soft brilliance, his fruit-trees, all arow, were outlining in shadow upon the walk, their slender limbs of wood scarce clothed by verdure; while the giant honeysuckle climbing on the house wall, exhaled delicious, sugared breaths, and seemed to cause to hover through the warm clear night a perfumed soul.

He began to breathe deep, drinking the air as drunkards drink their wine, and he walked slowly, being ravished, astounded, and almost oblivious of his niece.

As soon as he came into the open country he stopped to contemplate the whole plain, so inundated by this caressing radiance, so drowned in the tender and languishing charm of the serene nights. At every instant the frogs threw into space their short metallic notes, and the distant nightingales mingled with the seduction of the moonlight that fitful music of theirs which brings no thoughts but dreams, that light and vibrant melody of theirs which is composed for kisses.

The abbé continued his course, his courage failing, he knew not why. He felt, as it were, enfeebled, and suddenly exhausted; he had a great desire to sit down, to pause here, to praise God in all His works.

Down there, following the bends of the

little river, wound a great line of poplars. On and about the banks, wrapping all the tortuous watercourse with a kind of light, transparent wadding, hung suspended a fine mist, a white vapor, which the moon-rays crossed, and silvered, and caused to gleam.

The priest paused yet again, penetrated to the bottom of his soul by a strong and growing emotion.

And a doubt, a vague uneasiness, seized on him; he perceived that one of those questions which he sometimes put to himself, was now being born.

Why had God done this? Since the night is destined for sleep, for unconsciousness, for repose, for forgetfulness of everything, why, then, make it more charming than the day, sweeter than the dawns and the sunsets? And this slow seductive star, more poetical than the sun, and so discreet that it seems designed to light up things too delicate, too mysterious, for the great luminary,—why was it come to brighten all the shades?

Why did not the cleverest of all songsters go to rest like the others? And why did he set himself to singing in the vaguely troubling dark?

Why this half-veil over the world? Why these quiverings of the heart, this emotion of the soul, this languor of the body?

Why this display of seductions which mankind never sees, being asleep in bed? For whom was intended this sublime spectacle, this flood of poetry poured from heaven to earth?

And the abbé did not understand at all.

But now, see, down there along the edge of the field appeared two shadows walking side by side under the arched roof of the trees all soaked in glittering mist.

The man was the taller, and had his arm about his mistress's neck, and from time to time he kissed her on the forehead. They animated suddenly the lifeless landscape, which enveloped them like a divine frame made expressly for this. They seemed, these two, like one being, the being for whom was destined this calm and silent night; and they came on towards the priest like a living answer, the answer vouchsafed by his Master to his question.

He stood stock-still, quite overwhelmed, and with a beating heart. And he thought to see here some Bible story, like the loves of Ruth and Boaz, the accomplishment of the will of the Lord in one of those great scenes talked of in the holy books. Through his head began to hum the versicles of the Song of Songs, the ardent cries, the calls of the body, all the passionate poetry of that poem which burns with tenderness and love.

And he said to himself, "God perhaps has made such nights as this to clothe with the ideal the loves of men."

He withdrew before this couple who went ever arm in arm. For all that, it was really his niece; but now he asked himself if he had not been about to disobey God. And does not God indeed permit love, since He surrounds it visibly with splendor such as this?

And he fled, in a maze, almost ashamed, as if he had penetrated into a temple where he had not the right to go.

VIII.
THE CONFESSION.

THE CONFESSION.

MARGUÉRITE DE THÉRELLES was dying. Although but fifty-six, she seemed like seventy-five at least. She panted, paler than the sheets, shaken by dreadful shiverings, her face convulsed, her eyes haggard, as if she had seen some horrible thing.

Her eldest sister, Suzanne, six years older, sobbed on her knees beside the bed. A little table drawn close to the couch of the dying woman, and covered with a napkin, bore two lighted candles, the priest being momentarily expected to give extreme unction and the communion, which should be the last.

The apartment had that sinister aspect, that air of hopeless farewells, which belongs to the chambers of the dying. Medicine bottles stood about on the furniture, linen lay in the corners, pushed aside by foot or broom. The disordered chairs themselves seemed affrighted, as if they had run, in all the senses of the word. Death, the formidable, was there, hidden, waiting.

The story of the two sisters was very touching. It was quoted far and wide; it had made many eyes to weep.

Suzanne, the elder, had once been madly in love with a young man, who had also been in love with her. They were engaged, and were only waiting the day fixed for the contract, when Henry de Lampierre suddenly died.

The despair of the young girl was dreadful, and she vowed that she would never marry. She kept her word. She put on widow's weeds, which she never took off.

Then her sister, her little sister Marguérite, who was only twelve years old, came one morning to throw herself into the arms of the elder, and said: "Big Sister, I do not want thee to be unhappy. I do not want thee to cry all thy life. I will never leave thee, never, never! I—I, too, shall never marry. I shall stay with thee always, always, always!"

Suzanne, touched by the devotion of the child, kissed her, but did not believe.

Yet the little one, also, kept her word, and despite the entreaties of her parents, despite the supplications of the elder, she never married. She was pretty, very pretty; she refused many a young man who seemed to love her truly; and she never left her sister more.

They lived together all the days of their life, without ever being separated a single time. They went side by side, inseparably united. But Marguérite seemed always sad, oppressed, more melancholy than the elder, as though perhaps her sublime sacrifice had broken her spirit. She aged more quickly, had white hair from the age of thirty, and often suffering, seemed afflicted by some secret, gnawing trouble.

Now she was to be the first to die.

Since yesterday she was no longer able to

speak. She had only said, at the first glimmers of day-dawn:

"Go fetch Monsieur le Curé, the moment has come."

And she had remained since then upon her back, shaken with spasms, her lips agitated as though dreadful words were mounting from her heart without power of issue, her look mad with fear, terrible to see.

Her sister, torn by sorrow, wept wildly, her forehead resting on the edge of the bed, and kept repeating:

"Margot, my poor Margot, my little one!"

She had always called her, "Little One," just as the younger had always called her "Big Sister."

Steps were heard on the stairs. The door opened. A choir-boy appeared, followed by an old priest in a surplice. As soon as she perceived him, the dying woman, with one shudder, sat up, opened her lips, stammered two or three words, and began to scratch the sheet with her nails as if she had wished to make a hole.

The Abbé Simon approached, took her

hand, kissed her brow, and with a soft voice:

"God pardon thee, my child; have courage, the moment is now come, speak."

Then Marguérite, shivering from head to foot, shaking her whole couch with nervous movements, stammered:

"Sit down, Big Sister . . . listen."

The priest bent down towards Suzanne, who was still flung upon the bed's foot. He raised her, placed her in an arm-chair, and taking a hand of each of the sisters in one of his own, he pronounced:

"Lord, my God! Endue them with strength, cast Thy mercy upon them."

And Marguérite began to speak. The words issued from her throat one by one, raucous, with sharp pauses, as though very feeble.

"Pardon, pardon, Big Sister; oh, forgive! If thou knewest how I have had fear of this moment all my life . . ."

Suzanne stammered through her tears:

"Forgive thee what, Little One? Thou

hast given all to me, sacrificed everything; thou art an angel . . ."

But Marguérite interrupted her:

"Hush, hush! Let me speak . . . do not stop me. It is dreadful . . . let me tell all . . . to the very end, without flinching. Listen. Thou rememberest . . . thou rememberest . . . Henry . . ."

Suzanne trembled and looked at her sister. The younger continued:

"Thou must hear all, to understand. I was twelve years old, only twelve years old; thou rememberest well, is it not so? And I was spoiled, I did everything that I liked! Thou rememberest, surely, how they spoiled me? Listen. The first time that he came he had varnished boots. He got down from his horse at the great steps, and he begged pardon for his costume, but he came to bring some news to papa. Thou rememberest, is it not so? Don't speak—listen. When I saw him I was completely carried away, I found him so very beautiful; and I remained standing in a corner of the *salon* all the time that he was talking. Children are strange . . . and terrible. Oh yes . . . I have dreamed of all that.

"He came back again... several times... I looked at him with all my eyes, with all my soul... I was large of my age... and very much more knowing than any one thought. He came back often... I thought only of him. I said, very low:

"'Henry... Henry de Lampierre!'

"Then they said that he was going to marry thee. It was a sorrow; oh, Big Sister, a sorrow... a sorrow! I cried for three nights without sleeping. He came back every day, in the afternoon, after his lunch... thou rememberest, is it not so? Say nothing... listen. Thou madest him cakes which he liked... with meal, with butter and milk. Oh, I know well how. I could make them yet if it were needed. He ate them at one mouthful, and... and then he drank a glass of wine, and then he said, 'It is delicious.' Thou rememberest how he would say that?

"I was jealous, jealous! The moment of thy marriage approached. There were only two weeks more. I became crazy. I said to myself: 'He shall not marry Suzanne, no, I will not have it! It is I whom he will marry when I am grown up. I shall never find any one whom I love so much.' But one night, ten days before the contract, thou tookest a walk with him in front of the château by moonlight ... and there ... under the fir, under the great fir ... he kissed thee ... kissed ... holding thee in his two arms ... so long. Thou rememberest, is it not so? It was probably the first time ... yes ... Thou wast so pale when thou camest back to the *salon*.

"I had seen you two; I was there, in the shrubbery. I was angry! If I could I should have killed you both!

"I said to myself: 'He shall not marry Suzanne, never! He shall marry no one. I should be too unhappy.' And all of a sudden I began to hate him dreadfully.

"Then, dost thou know what I did? Listen. I had seen the gardener making little balls to kill strange dogs. He pounded up a bottle with a stone and put the powdered glass in a little ball of meat.

"I took a little medicine bottle that mamma had; I broke it small with a hammer, and I hid the glass in my pocket. It was a shining powder ... The next day, as soon as you had made the little cakes ... I split them with a knife and I put in the glass ... He ate three of them ... I too, I ate one ... I threw the other six into the pond. The two swans died three days after ... Dost thou remember? Oh, say nothing ... listen, listen. I, I alone did not die ... but I have always been sick. Listen ... He died—thou knowest well ... listen ... that, that is nothing. It is afterwards, later ... always ... the worst ... listen.

"My life, all my life ... what torture! I said to myself: 'I will never leave my sister. And at the hour of death I will tell her all ...' There! And ever since, I have always thought of that moment when I should tell thee all. Now it is come. It is terrible. Oh ... Big Sister!

"I have always thought, morning and evening, by night and by day, 'Some time I must tell her that ...' I waited ... What agony! ... It is done. Say nothing. Now I am afraid ... am afraid ... oh, I am afraid. If I am going to see him again, soon, when I am dead. See him again ... think of it! The first! Before thou! I shall not dare.

I must... I am going to die... I want you to forgive me. I want it... I cannot go off to meet him without that. Oh, tell her to forgive me, Monsieur le Curé, tell her... I implore you to do it. I cannot die without that..."

She was silent, and remained panting, always scratching the sheet with her withered nails.

Suzanne had hidden her face in her hands, and did not move. She was thinking of him whom she might have loved so long! What a good life they should have lived together! She saw him once again in that vanished by-gone time, in that old past which was put out forever. The beloved dead—how they tear your hearts! Oh, that kiss, his only kiss! She had hidden it in her soul. And after it nothing, nothing more her whole life long!

All of a sudden the priest stood straight, and, with strong vibrant voice, he cried:

"Mademoiselle Suzanne, your sister is dying!"

Then Suzanne, opening her hands, showed her face soaked with tears, and throwing herself upon her sister, she kissed her with all her might, stammering:

"I forgive thee, I forgive thee, Little One."

IX.
ON THE JOURNEY.

ON THE JOURNEY.

Since leaving Cannes the carriage had been full; and being all acquainted, we conversed together. As we passed Tarascon some one said, "It is here the murders happen." And we began to talk of that mysterious assassin who has never been caught, and who from time to time during the last two years has offered up to himself some traveller's life. Every one hazarded suppositions, every one gave his opinion; the women looked shiveringly at the sombre night behind the panes, fearing to see the head of a man show suddenly in the doorway. And we began to tell dreadful stories of terrible adventures, of some tête-à-tête with a madman in an express, of hours passed opposite suspicious-looking persons, quite alone.

All the men had stories "on their honor," all had intimidated, knocked down, and choked some malefactor in surprising circumstances, and with admirable boldness and presence of mind. A physician, who passed each winter in the South, wished in his turn to tell a tale.

"I," said he, "have never had the chance to try my courage in an affair of that sort; but I knew a woman, one of my patients, who is now dead, to whom there happened the strangest thing in the world, and also the most mysterious and the most affecting.

"She was a Russian, the Countess Marie Baranow, a very great lady, of exquisite beauty. You all know how beautiful the Russian women are, or at least how beautiful they seem to us, with their fine nostrils, with their delicate mouths, with their eyes of an indefinable color—a sort of blue-gray, set close together—and with that grace of theirs which is cold and a little hard. They have about them something naughty and seductive, something haughty and gentle, something tender and severe, which is altogether charming to a Frenchman. It is perhaps, however, only the difference of race and type which makes me see so much.

"For several years her doctor had perceived that she was threatened with a malady of the chest, and had been trying to induce her to go to the South of France; but she obstinately refused to leave St. Petersburg. Finally, last autumn, the physician gave her up as lost, and so informed her husband, who at once ordered his wife to leave for Mentone.

"She took the train, alone in her carriage, her servants occupying another compartment. She leaned against the door-way, a little sad, watching the country and the passing villages, feeling herself in life so lonely, so abandoned, without children, almost without relatives, with a husband whose love was dead, and who, not coming with her, had just thrown her off to the end of the world as he would send to the hospital a valet who was sick.

"At each station her body-servant Ivan came to ask if anything was wanted by his mistress. He was an old servant, blindly devoted, ready to carry out any order which she might give.

"The night fell, the train rolled onward at full speed. She was much unstrung, she could not sleep. Suddenly she took the idea of counting the money which her husband had given her at the last moment, in French gold. She opened her little bag, and emptied the shining flood of metal upon her knees.

But all of a sudden a breath of cold air struck her in the face. She raised her head in surprise. The door had just swung open. The Countess Marie, in desperation, brusquely threw a shawl over the money which was spread upon her knees, and waited. Some seconds passed, then a man appeared, bareheaded, wounded in the hand, panting, in evening dress. He shut the door again, sat down, looked at his neighbor with glittering eyes, then wrapped a handkerchief round his wrist, from which the blood was flowing.

"The young countess felt herself grow weak with fright. This man had certainly seen her counting her gold, and he was come to murder and to rob.

"He kept staring at her, breathless, his face convulsed, ready, no doubt, to make a spring.

"He said, suddenly:

"'Have no fear, madame!'

"She answered nothing, being unable to open her mouth, hearing her heart beat and her ears hum.

"He continued:

"'I am not a criminal, madame.'

"She still said nothing, but, in a brusque movement which she made, her knees came close together, and her gold began to flow down upon the carpet as water flows from a gutter.

"The man, surprised, looked at this rivulet of metal, and suddenly he stooped to pick up the money.

"She rose in a mad fright, casting all her treasure to the ground, and she ran to the door to throw herself out upon the track. But he understood what she was about to do, rushed forward, caught her in his arms, made her sit down by force, and holding her wrists: 'Listen, madame, I am not a criminal, and the proof is that I am going to pick up this money and give it back to you. But I am a lost man, a dead man, unless you help me to cross the frontier. I cannot tell you more. In one hour we shall be at the last Russian station; in one hour and twenty minutes we shall pass the boundary of the empire. If you do not rescue me I am lost. And yet, madame, I have neither killed nor stolen, nor done anything against my honor. I swear it to you. I cannot tell you more.'

"And getting down on his knees, he picked up the gold, looking even for the last pieces, which had rolled far under the seats. Then, when the little leather bag was once more full, he returned it to his neighbor without adding a word, and again he went and sat in the other corner of the carriage.

"They no longer stirred, either one or the

other. She remained motionless and dumb, still fainting with terror, then little by little growing more at ease. As for him, he did not make a gesture, a movement; he sat straight, his eyes fastened before him, very pale, as though he had been dead. From time to time she looked at him suddenly, and as suddenly looked away. He was a man about thirty, very handsome, with every appearance of a gentleman.

"The train ran through the darkness, cast rending cries across the night, sometimes slackened its pace, then went off again at full speed. But suddenly it slowed, whistled several times, and stopped.

"Ivan appeared at the door to get his orders.

"The Countess Marie, with a trembling voice, considered her strange companion for the last time, then said to her servant, with a brusque voice:

"'Ivan, you are to return to the count; I have no more need of you.'

"The man, speechless, opened his enormous eyes. He stammered:

"'But—Barine!'

"She continued:

"'No, you are not to come; I have changed my mind. I desire that you remain in Russia. Here is money to return. Give me your cap and your cloak.'

"The old servant, quite bewildered, bared his head and held out his cloak. He always obeyed without reply, being well accustomed to the sudden wishes and the irresistible caprices of his masters. And he withdrew, the tears in his eyes.

"The train went on, running towards the frontier.

"Then the Countess Marie said to her neighbor:

"'These things are for you, monsieur; you are Ivan, my servant. I add only one condition to what I do: it is that you shall never speak to me, that you shall not address me a single word, either to thank me or for any purpose whatever.'

"The unknown bowed without uttering a word.

"Very soon they came to a stop once more, and officials in uniform visited the train. The countess offered them her papers, and pointing to the man seated at the back of the carriage:

"'My servant, Ivan. Here is his passport.'

"The train went on.

"During the whole night they remained in tête-à-tête, both silent.

"In the morning, when they stopped at a German station, the unknown got down; then, standing straight in the door-way:

"'Forgive my breaking my promise, madame; but I have deprived you of your servant, it is right that I should fill his place. Have you need of anything?'

"She answered, coldly:

"'Go and find my maid.'

"He went to do so, then disappeared.

"When she got out of the carriage at some restaurant or other, she perceived him from a distance looking at her. They reached Mentone."

The doctor was silent a second, then resumed:

"One day, as I was receiving my patients

in my office, I saw enter a tall young fellow, who said to me:

"'Doctor, I come to ask news about the Countess Marie Baranow. I am, although she does not know me, a friend of her husband.'

"I replied:

"'She is doomed. She will never go back to Russia.'

"And the man suddenly commenced to sob, then he got up and went out, reeling like a drunkard.

"The same night I told the countess that a stranger had come to inquire from me about her health. She seemed moved, and told me all the story which I have just told you. She added:

"'That man, whom I do not know at all, now follows me like my shadow, I meet him every time I go out; he looks at me after a strange fashion, but he has never spoken.'

"She reflected, then added:

"'See, I would wager he is under my windows.'

"She left her easy-chair, went to pull back

the curtains, and, sure enough, she showed me the man who had come to see me, now seated there on a bench upon the promenade, his eyes lifted towards the hotel. He perceived us, rose, and went off without once turning his head.

"And from that time forward I assisted at a surprising and sorrowful thing—at the silent love of these two beings, who did not even know one another.

"He loved her with the affection of an animal who has been saved, and who is grateful and devoted unto death. He came each day to say to me: 'How is she?' understanding that I had divined the secret. And he cried when he had seen her pass each day feebler and paler.

"She said to me:

"'I have spoken but a single time to that strange man, and it seems to me as if I had known him for twenty years.'

"And when they met, she would return his bow with a grave and charming smile. I could see that she was happy—she, the abandoned, the doomed—I could see that she was happy to be loved like this, with such respect and such constancy, with such exaggerated poetry, with this devotion which was ready for all things. And notwithstanding, faithful to her mystical resolve, she wildly refused to receive him, to know his name, to speak with him. She said: 'No, no, that would spoil for me this curious friendship. We must remain strangers one to the other.'

"As for him, he also was certainly a kind of Don Quixote, because he made no attempt to approach her. He meant to keep to the end the absurd promise of never speaking, which he had made her in the railway carriage.

"Often, during her weary hours of weakness, she rose from her long chair, and went to open the curtains a little way to see if he was there, beneath her window. And when she had seen him, always motionless upon his bench, she went back and lay down with a smile upon her lips.

"She died one day about ten o'clock. As I was leaving the hotel he came up to me with a distracted face; he had already heard the news.

"'I should like to see her, for one second, in your presence,' said he.

"I took him by the arm and went back into the house.

"When he was before the couch of the dead he seized her hand and kissed it with an endless kiss, then escaped like a madman."

The doctor again was silent; then continued:

"This is certainly the strangest railway adventure that I know. It must also be said that men take sometimes the wildest freaks."

A woman murmured, half aloud:

"Those two people were not so crazy as you think. They were—they were—"

But she could not speak further, she was crying so. As we changed the conversation to calm her, we never knew what she had wished to say.

X.
THE BEGGAR.

THE BEGGAR.

He had known better days, despite his wretchedness and his infirmity.

At the age of fifteen he had had both legs crushed by a carriage on the high-road of Yarville. Since then he begged, dragging himself along the roads, across the farm-yards, balanced on his crutches, which had made his shoulders mount as high as his ears, so that his head seemed sunk between two mountains.

A child found in a ditch by the curé of Les Billettes, on All Souls' Eve, and baptized, for that reason, Nicolas Toussaint, he had been brought up on charity, and had remained a stranger to all instruction. It was after the village baker had given him several glasses of brandy to drink that he had lamed his legs. And since then, a laughing-stock and a vagabond, he knew of nothing else to do but to hold out his hand and beg.

Formerly the Baroness d'Avary had allowed him to sleep in a kind of niche full of straw beside the hen-house at the farm, which was under the castle walls; and on bad days he was sure of finding a piece of bread and a glass of cider in her kitchen. He also often got a few sous thrown him by the old lady from the top of her steps or from the windows of her chamber. Now she was dead.

In the villages they hardly gave him anything: they knew him too well; this forty years they were tired of seeing him carrying about his ragged and deformed body from hut to hut on his two wooden joints. And yet he did not want to go away, because he knew of nothing else on earth but this corner of a country, these three or four hamlets in which he had dragged about his miserable life. He had set a boundary to his beggarhood, and he would never have thought of passing the limits which he was not accustomed to cross.

He did not know whether the world extended very much farther beyond the trees which had always bounded his sight. He never asked himself that. And when the peasants, tired of always meeting him on the borders of their fields or along their ditches, cried at him, "Why don't you go to the other villages instead of forever limping round here?" he made no reply, and went off seized with a vague fear of the unknown, with the fear of a poor wretch who was confusedly afraid of a thousand things —of strange faces, of insults, of the suspicious looks of people who did not know him, and of the gendarmes, who went two by two along the roads, making him dive by instinct into the thickets or behind the piles of pounded stones.

When he saw their uniforms at a distance, glittering in the sun, he suddenly discovered marvellous agility, the agility of a monster who tries to gain some hiding-place. He dropped from his crutches, let himself fall as a rag falls, rolled himself into a ball, and became quite small, invisible, as close to the ground as a hare in her form, confounding his brown tatters with the earth.

He had, however, never had any trouble with the gendarmes. And yet he carried this in his blood, as though he had inherited this terror and this trick from his parents, whom he had never known.

He had no place of refuge, no roof of his own, no covering, no shelter. He slept anywhere in summer, and in winter he slipped under the barns or into the stables with remarkable address. He always stole out early in the morning before he should be perceived. He knew all the holes by which buildings could be entered. And the use of his crutches having given his arms extraordinary strength, he sometimes climbed by sheer force of his wrists up into the haylofts, where he would remain four or five days without moving, provided in going his round he had secured food enough to keep him alive.

In the midst of men, he lived like the beasts of the wood, knowing no one, loving no one, exciting only among the peasants a sort of indifferent disdain and resigned hostility. They nicknamed him "The Bell," because indeed he did swing between his two stakes of wood like a bell between its supports.

For two days he had eaten nothing. They no longer gave him anything at all. They meant to be rid of him at last. The peasant wives, on their door-steps, cried afar off, on seeing him coming:

"Will you begone, you rascal! I gave you a piece of bread only three days ago!"

And he pivoted upon his props, and took himself off to the next house, where they received him after the same fashion.

From one door to the other the women declared:

"All very well, but we can't feed this sluggard all the year round."

And yet every day the sluggard had need to eat.

He had gone the round in Saint Hilaire, Yarville, and Les Billettes without getting a centime or an old crust. His last hope was at Tournolles; but he must go two leagues on the high-road, and he felt himself too exhausted to drag himself farther, having a stomach as empty as his pocket.

Nevertheless, he set himself to walking.

It was in December. A cold wind ran on the fields and whistled through the bare branches. And the clouds galloped across the low and sombre sky, hastening one knows not whither. The cripple went slowly, lifting his supports from their place one after the other with a painful effort, wedging himself up on his one remaining twisted leg, which was terminated by a club-foot shod with a clout.

From time to time he sat down on the edge of the ditch and rested several minutes. Hunger threw a confused and heavy distress into his soul. He had only one thought: "to eat," but how he did not know.

For three hours he toiled over the long road; then, when he perceived the trees of the village, he hastened his steps.

The first peasant whom he met, and of whom he asked alms, replied to him:

"So here you are again, you old rogue! Sha'n't we ever be rid of you?"

And "The Bell" went on. From door to door they used him roughly, they sent him away without giving him anything. He continued his round, notwithstanding, patient and obstinate. He did not receive a sou.

Then he visited the farm-houses, reeling over the ground soft with rain, so weak that he could hardly lift his sticks. Everywhere they hunted him off. It was one of those cold, sad days when hearts are shut, when minds grow angry, when the soul is sombre, when the hand does not open to succor or to give.

When he had made the tour of all the houses which he knew, he went and threw himself down in the corner of a dry ditch beside the farm-yard of Maître Chiquet. He "unhooked" himself, as people said, to express the manner in which he let himself fall from his high crutches, making them slip from under his arms. And he remained for a long time motionless, tortured by hunger, but too much of an animal to really penetrate the depths of his unfathomable misery.

He awaited, he knew not what, with that vague sense of expectation which ever persists within us. He waited in the corner of that farm-yard under the icy wind, for the mysterious help which we always hope from the sky or from men, without asking ourselves how or why, or through whom it is to come. A flock of black chickens passed by, searching their subsistence in the earth, the nourisher of all. At every instant, with one stroke of the beak, they picked up a grain or an invisible insect, then continued their slow and steady search.

"The Bell" regarded them without thinking of anything at all; then, rather in his stomach than in his brain, there came to him a feeling rather than an idea that one of these creatures broiled over a fire of dead wood would be good to eat.

The suspicion that he was about to commit a theft did not occur to him. He took a stone which lay within reach of his hand, and being adroit, he threw it and fairly killed the chicken which was nearest by. The creature fell upon its side, moving its wings. The others fled away, balanced upon their slender feet. And "The Bell," climbing his crutches once more, set off to pick up his game with movements like those of the chickens.

Just as he arrived beside the little black body stained with blood about its head, he received a terrible blow in the back which made him drop his sticks and sent him rolling ten paces before them. And Maître Chiquet, in a rage, precipitating himself upon the marauder, thrashed him soundly, pounding with fist and knee all over the body of the defenceless cripple, like a madman, or like a peasant who has been robbed.

The farm servants arrived in their turn, and, with their master, fell to beating the beggar. Then, when they were tired, they picked him up and carried him off, and shut him up in the wood-house while they went to fetch the gendarmes.

"The Bell," half-dead, bleeding, and torn with hunger, remained lying on the ground. Evening came, then night, then daybreak. All this time he had eaten nothing.

Towards mid-day the gendarmes appeared and opened the door with great precaution, expecting a resistance, since Maître Chiquet made out that he had been attacked by the beggar, and had only defended himself with the greatest difficulty.

The corporal cried:

"Come, get up!"

But "The Bell" could no longer move; he tried, indeed, to hoist himself upon his sticks, but he did not succeed. They thought it was a feint, a trick, or the ugly temper of a malefactor, and the two armed men, seizing him roughly, planted him by force upon his crutches.

Fear had taken hold of him, the fear which the game has before the hunter, which the mouse has in presence of the cat. By superhuman efforts he managed to remain upright.

"Forward!" said the corporal. He walked. All the people of the farm were there to see him off. The women shook their fists; the men jeered and insulted him: he was caught at last! a good riddance.

He departed between his two guardians. He found enough energy of desperation to drag himself along till evening. He was brutalized, not even knowing what was happening to him, too much frightened to understand.

The people whom they met stopped to see him go by, and the peasants murmured:

"It is some robber!"

They arrived, towards night, at the capital of the district. He had never come as far as that. He did not even figure to himself what was going on, nor what might be about to happen. All these terrible and unexpected things, these shapes of unknown people, and these strange houses, struck him with consternation.

He did not utter a word, having nothing to say, for he no longer understood anything. Moreover, since for so many years he had conversed with no one, he had almost lost the use of his tongue; and his thoughts also were too confused to formulate themselves in speech.

They shut him up in the town jail. The gendarmes did not think of his needing food, and they left him till the next day.

But when they came to examine him, early in the morning, they found him dead, upon the ground. What a surprise!

XI.

A GHOST.

A GHOST.

We were talking of Processes of Sequestration, apropos of a recent law-case. It was towards the end of a friendly evening, in an ancient mansion in the Rue de Grenelle, and each one had his story, his story which he affirmed to be true.

Then the old Marquis de la Tour-Samuel, who was eighty-two years old, rose, and went and leaned upon the mantle-piece. He said, with a voice which shook a little:

"I too, I know a strange story, so strange that it has simply possessed my life. It is fifty-six years since that adventure happened, yet not a month passes without my seeing it all again in dreams. That day has left a mark, an imprint of fear, stamped on me, do you understand? Yes, for ten minutes I suffered such horrible terror that from that hour to this a sort of constant dread has rested on my soul. Unexpected noises make me tremble all over; objects which in the shades of evening I do not well distinguish cause me a mad desire to escape. The fact is, I am afraid of the night.

"No! I admit I should never have confessed this before arriving at my present age. But I can say what I like now. When a man is eighty-two years old it is permitted him to be afraid of imaginary dangers. And in the face of real ones I have never drawn back, *mesdames*.

"The affair so disturbed my spirit, and produced in me so profound, so mysterious, so dreadful a sense of trouble, that I have never even told it. I have kept it in the intimate recesses of my heart, in that corner where we hide our bitter and our shameful secrets, and all those unspeakable stories of weaknesses which we have committed but which we cannot confess.

"I shall tell you the tale exactly as it

happened, without trying to explain it. Certainly it can be explained — unless we assume that for an hour I was mad. But no, I was not mad, and I will give you the proof of it. Imagine what you like. Here are the plain facts:

"It was in the month of July, 1827. I found myself in garrison at Rouen.

"One day, as I was taking a walk upon the quay, I met a man whom I thought I recognized, although I did not remember exactly who he might be. I instinctively made a motion to stop. The stranger noticed the gesture, looked at me, and fell into my arms.

"It was a friend of my youth whom I had once loved dearly. The five years since I had seen him seemed to have aged him fifty. His hair was quite white; and when he walked he stooped as if exhausted. He understood my surprise, and told me about his life. He had been broken by a terrible sorrow.

"He had fallen madly in love with a very young girl, and he had married her with a kind of joyful ecstasy. But after one single year of superhuman happiness, she had suddenly died of a trouble at the heart, slain, no doubt, by love itself.

"He had left his château the very day of the funeral, and had come to reside in his hôtel at Rouen. He was now living there, solitary and desperate, preyed on by anguish, and so miserable that his only thought was suicide.

"'Now that I've found you again,' said he, 'I shall ask you to do me a great service. It is to go out to the château and bring me some papers of which I stand in urgent need. They are in the secretary in my room, in *our* room. I cannot intrust this commission to an inferior, or to a man of business, because I desire impenetrable discretion and absolute silence. And as to myself, I would not go back to that house for anything in the world.

"'I will give you the key of that chamber, which I closed myself when I went away. And I will give you the key of the secretary. Besides that, you shall have a line from me to my gardener, which will make you free of the château. But come and breakfast with me to-morrow, and we can talk about all that.'

"I promised to do him this service. It was indeed a mere excursion for me, since his estate lay only about five leagues from Rouen, and I could get there on horseback in an hour.

"I was with him at ten o'clock the next morning. We breakfasted alone together; yet he did not say twenty words. He begged me to forgive him for his silence. The thought of the visit which I was about to make to that chamber where his happiness lay dead, overwhelmed him completely, said he to me. And for a fact, he did seem strangely agitated and preoccupied, as if a mysterious struggle were passing in his soul.

"Finally, however, he explained to me exactly what I must do. It was quite simple. I must secure two packages of letters and a bundle of papers which were shut up in the first drawer on the right of the desk of which I had the key. He added:

"'I don't need to ask you not to look at them.'

"I was almost wounded by this, and I told him so a little hotly. He stammered:

"'Forgive me, I suffer so much.'

"And he fell to weeping.

"I left him about one o'clock, to accomplish my mission.

"It was brilliant weather, and I trotted fast across the fields, listening to the songs of the larks and the regular ring of my sabre on my boot.

"Next I entered the forest and walked my horse. Branches of trees caressed my face; and sometimes I would catch a leaf in my teeth, and chew it eagerly, in one of those ecstasies at being alive which fill you, one knows not why, with a tumultuous and almost elusive happiness, with a kind of intoxication of strength.

"On approaching the château, I looked in my pocket for the note which I had for the gardener, and I found to my astonishment that it was sealed. I was so surprised and irritated that I came near returning at once, without acquitting myself of my errand. But I reflected that I should in that case display a susceptibility which would be in bad taste. And, moreover, in his trouble, my friend might have sealed the note unconsciously.

"The manor looked as though it had been deserted these twenty years. How the gate, which was open and rotten, held up, was hard to tell. Grass covered the walks. You no longer made out the borders of the lawn.

"At the noise which I made by kicking a shutter with my foot, an old man came out of a side door and seemed stupefied at the sight. I leaped to the ground and delivered my letter. He read it, read it again, turned it round, looked at me askance, put the paper in his pocket, and remarked:

"'Well! What do you want?'

"I answered, sharply:

"'You ought to know, since you have received the orders of your master in that letter. I want to enter the château.'

"He seemed overwhelmed. He said:

"'So, you are going into... into his room?'

"I began to grow impatient.

"'*Parbleu!* But do you mean to put me through an examination, my good man?'

"He stammered:

"'No . . . monsieur . . . only . . . it has not been opened since . . . since the . . . death. If you will wait five minutes, I will go . . . go and see whether . . .'

"I interrupted him, angrily:

"'Come, come! Are you playing with me? You know you can't get in. I have the key.'

"He had nothing more to say.

"'Well, monsieur, I will show you the way.'

"'Show me the staircase, and leave me alone. I shall find the room well enough without you.'

"'But . . . monsieur . . . but . . .'

"This time I went fairly into a rage:

"'Be quiet! do you hear? Or you will have to reckon with me.'

"I pushed him violently aside, and I penetrated into the house.

"First I crossed the kitchen, then two little rooms inhabited by the fellow and his wife. I next passed into a great hall, I climbed the stairs, and I recognized the door as indicated by my friend.

"I opened it without trouble, and entered.

"The room was so dark that at first I hardly made out anything. I paused, struck by that mouldy and lifeless odor so peculiar to apartments which are uninhabited and condemned, and, as you might say, dead. Then, little by little, my eyes became accustomed to the gloom, and I saw, clearly enough, a great apartment all in disorder; the bed without sheets, yet with its mattress and its pillows, one of which bore the deep impress of an elbow or a head, as if some one had just lain on it.

"The chairs seemed all in confusion. I noticed that a door (into a closet, no doubt) had remained half open.

"I went first to the window to let in some light, and I opened it; but the iron fastenings of the outside shutter were so rusty that I could not make them yield.

"I even tried to break them with my sabre, but without success. And as I was growing angry at these useless efforts, and as my eyes had at last perfectly accustomed themselves to the darkness, I gave up the hope of seeing more clearly, and I went to the desk.

"I seated myself in an arm-chair, lowered the shelf, and opened the indicated drawer. It was full to the top. I needed only three packets, which I knew how to tell. And I set myself to looking.

"I was straining my eyes to decipher the inscriptions, when behind me I thought I heard a slight rustle. I paid no heed to it, thinking that a current of air had made some of the hangings stir. But, in a minute, another almost imperceptible movement caused a singular, unpleasant little shiver to pass over my skin. It was so stupid to be even in the least degree nervous that I would not turn round, being ashamed for myself in my own presence. I had then just discovered the second of the bundles which I wanted. And now, just as I lit upon the third, the breath of a great and painful sigh against my shoulder caused me to give one mad leap two yards away. In my start I had turned quite round, with my hand upon my sabre, and if I had not felt it by my side I should certainly have run like a coward.

"A tall woman dressed in white stood looking at me from behind the arm-chair in which, a second before, I had been sitting.

"Such a shudder ran through my limbs that I almost fell backward! Oh, no one who has not felt it can understand a dreadful yet foolish fear like that. The soul fairly melts away; you are conscious of a heart no longer; the whole body becomes as lax as a sponge; and you would say that everything within you was falling to pieces.

"I do not believe in ghosts at all.—Well, I tell you that at that moment I grew faint under the hideous fear of the dead. And from the irresistible anguish caused by supernatural terrors I suffered, oh, I suffered in a few seconds more than I have done all the rest of my life.

"If she had not spoken I should perhaps have died! But she did speak; she spoke in a sweet and dolorous voice which made my nerves quiver. I should not venture to say that I became master of myself and that I recovered my reason. No. I was so frightened that I no longer knew what I was doing; but a kind of personal dignity which

I have in me, and also a little professional pride, enabled me to keep up an honorable countenance almost in spite of myself. I posed for my own benefit, and for hers, no doubt—for hers, woman or spectre, whatever she might be. I analyzed all this later, because, I assure you, that at the instant of the apparition I did not do much thinking. I was afraid.

"She said:

"'Oh, monsieur, you can do me a great service!'

"I tried to answer, but it was simply impossible for me to utter a word. A vague sound issued from my throat.

"She continued:

"'Will you do it? You can save me, cure me. I suffer dreadfully. I suffer, oh, I suffer!'

"And she sat down gently in my armchair. She looked at me:

"'Will you do it?'

"I made the sign 'yes' with my head, for my voice was gone.

"Then she held out to me a tortoise-shell comb and she murmured:

"'Comb my hair; oh, comb my hair! That will cure me. They must comb my hair. Look at my head. How I suffer! And my hair, how it hurts me!'

"Her hair, which was loose and long and very black (as it seemed to me), hung down over the arm-chair's back and touched the ground.

"Why did I do that? Why, all shivering, did I receive the comb? And why did I take into my hands that long hair, which gave my skin a feeling of atrocious cold, as if I were touching serpents? I do not know.

"That feeling still clings about my fingers. And when I think of it I tremble.

"I combed her. I handled, I know not how, that icy hair. I twisted it. I bound it and unbound it. I plaited it as we plait a horse's mane. She sighed, bent her head, seemed happy.

"Suddenly she said to me, 'I thank you!' caught the comb out of my hands, and fled through the half-open door which I had noticed.

"For several seconds after I was left

alone, I experienced that wild trouble of the soul which one feels after a nightmare from which one has just awakened. Then at last I recovered my senses; I ran to the window, and I broke the shutters open with violent blows.

"A flood of daylight entered. I rushed upon the door by which she had disappeared. I found it shut and immovable.

"Then a fever of flight seized on me, a panic, a real panic such as overcomes an army. I caught up roughly the three packets of letters from the open desk; I crossed the room at a run; I took the steps of the staircase four at a time; I found myself outside, I don't know how; and, perceiving my horse ten paces off, I mounted him with one leap and went off at full gallop.

"I did not pause till I was before the door of my lodgings in Rouen. Throwing the reins to my orderly, I escaped to my room, where I locked myself in to think.

"And then for an hour I kept anxiously asking whether I had not been the sport of some hallucination. I had certainly had one of those incomprehensible nervous shocks, one of those affections of the brain which dwarf the miracles to which the supernatural owes its power.

"And I had almost come to believe it was a delusion, an error of my senses, when I drew near the window, and my eyes lit by chance upon my breast. My dolman was covered with long woman's hairs which had rolled themselves around the buttons!

"I took them one by one and I threw them out of the window, with trembling in my fingers.

"Then I called my orderly. I felt too much moved, too much troubled, to go near my friend that day. And I wished also to ponder carefully what I should say to him about all this.

"I had the letters taken to his house. He gave the soldier a receipt. He asked many questions about me, and my soldier told him that I was unwell, that I had had a sun-stroke—something. He seemed uneasy.

"I went to him the next day, early in the morning, having resolved to tell him the truth. He had gone out the evening before, and had not come back.

"I returned in the course of the day. They had seen nothing of him. I waited a week. He did not reappear. Then I informed the police. They searched for him everywhere without discovering a trace of his passing or of his final retreat.

"A minute inspection of the abandoned château was instituted. Nothing suspicious was discovered.

"No sign that a woman had been hidden there revealed itself.

"The inquiry proving fruitless, the search was interrupted.

"And for fifty-six years I have learned nothing. I know nothing more."

XII.
LITTLE SOLDIER.

LITTLE SOLDIER

Every Sunday, as soon as they were free, the two little soldiers set off.

On leaving the barracks they turned to the right; went through Courbevoie with long quick steps, as though they were on a march; then, having left the houses behind them, they followed at a calmer gait the bare and dusty high-road which leads to Bezons.

Being little and thin, they looked quite lost in their coats, which were too big and too long. The sleeves hung down over their hands, and they were much bothered by their enormous red breeches, which compelled them to walk wide. Under their stiff, high shakos their faces seemed like mere nothings — two poor, hollow Breton faces, simple in an almost animal simplicity, and with blue eyes which were gentle and calm.

During the walk they never spoke. They went straight on, each with the same idea in his head as the other. It stood them in place of conversation, for the fact is that just inside the little wood near Les Champioux they had found a place which reminded them of their own country, and it was only there that they felt happy.

When they came under the trees where the roads from Colombes and from Chatou cross, they would take off their heavy shakos and wipe their foreheads.

They always stopped a little while on the Bezons bridge to look at the Seine. They would remain there two or three minutes, bent double, leaning on the parapet. Or sometimes they would gaze out over the great basin of Argenteuil, where the skiffs might be seen scudding, with their white, slanted sails, recalling perhaps the look of the Breton water, the harbor of Vannes, near which they lived, and the fishing-boats standing out across the Morbihan to the open sea.

As soon as they had crossed the Seine they bought their provisions from the sausage merchant, the baker, and the seller of the wine of the country. A piece of blood-pudding, four sous' worth of bread, and a litre of "petit bleu" constituted the provisions, which they carried off in their handkerchiefs. But after they had left this village they now went very slowly forward, and they began to talk.

In front of them a barren plain strewn with clumps of trees led to the wood, to the little wood which had seemed to them to resemble the one at Kermarivan. Grain-fields and hay-fields bordered the narrow path, which lost itself in this young greenness of the crops, and Jean Kerderen would always say to Luc le Ganidec:

"It looks like it does near Plounivon."

"Yes; exactly."

They went onward, side by side, their spirits suffused with vague memories of their own country, filled with awakened images— images as naïve as the pictures on the colored broadsheets which you buy for a penny. And they kept recognizing, as it were, now a corner of a field, a hedge, a bit of moorland, now a cross-roads, now a granite cross.

Then, too, they would always stop beside a certain landmark, a great stone, because it looked something like the cromlech at Locneuven.

On arriving at the first clump of trees Luc le Ganidec every Sunday cut a switch, a hazel switch, and began gently to peel off the bark, thinking meanwhile of the folk there at home.

Jean Kerderen carried the provisions.

From time to time Luc mentioned a name, or recalled some doing of their childhood in a few brief words, which caused long thoughts. And their own country, their dear distant country, repossessed them little by little, seized upon them, and sent to them from afar her shapes, her sounds, her well-known prospects, her odors—odors of the green lands where the salt sea-air was blowing.

They were no longer conscious of the exhalations of the Parisian stables on which the earth of the *banlieue* fattens, but of the perfume of the flowering broom, which the salt breeze of the open sea plucks and bears away. And the sails of the boats, appearing above the river-banks, seemed to them the sails of the coasting vessels perceived beyond the great plain which extended from their homes to the very margin of the waves.

They went with short steps, Luc le Ganidec and Jean Kerderen, content and sad, haunted by a sweet melancholy, by the lingering, penetrating sorrow of a caged animal who remembers.

And by the time that Luc had stripped the slender wand of its bark they arrived at the corner of the wood where every Sunday they took breakfast.

They found the two bricks which they had hidden in the thicket, and they kindled a little fire of branches, over which to roast their blood-pudding at the end of a bayonet.

And when they had breakfasted, eaten their bread to the last crumb, and drunk their wine to the last drop, they remained seated side by side upon the grass, saying nothing, their eyes on the distance, their eyelids drooping, their fingers crossed as at mass, their red legs stretched out beside the poppies of the field. And the leather of their shakos and the brass of their buttons glittered in the ardent sun, and made the larks, which sang and hovered above their heads, stop short.

About mid-day they began to turn their eyes from time to time in the direction of the village of Bezons, because the girl with the cow was coming.

· She passed by them every Sunday on her way to milk and change the position of her cow — the only cow of this district which ever went out of the stable to grass. It pastured in a narrow field along the edge of wood a little farther on.

They soon perceived the girl, the only human being who came walking across the land. And they felt themselves rejoiced by the brilliant reflections thrown off by her tin milk-pail under the flame of the sun. They never talked about her. They were simply glad to see her, without understanding why.

She was a great strong wench with red

hair, burned by the heat of sunny days, a great sturdy wench of the environs of Paris.

Once, finding them again seated in the same place, she said:

"Good-morning. You two are always here, aren't you?"

Luc le Ganidec, the bolder, stammered:

"Yes; we come to rest."

That was all. But the next Sunday she laughed on seeing them, laughed with a protecting benevolence and a feminine keenness which knew well enough that they were bashful. And she asked:

"What are you doing there? Are you trying to see the grass grow?"

Luc was cheered up by this, and smiled likewise: "Maybe we are."

She continued: "*Hein!* That's pretty slow work."

He answered, still laughing: "Well, yes, it is."

She went on. But coming back with a milk-pail full of milk, she stopped again before them, and said:

"Would you like a drop? It will taste like home."

With her instinctive feeling that they were of the same peasant race as she, being herself also far away from home perhaps, she had divined and touched the spot.

They were both touched. Then, with some difficulty, she managed to make a little milk run into the neck of the glass bottle in which they carried their wine. And Luc drank first, with little swallows, stopping every minute to see whether he had drunk more than his half. Then he handed the bottle to Jean.

She stood upright before them, her hands on her hips, her pail on the ground at her feet, glad at the pleasure which she had given.

Then she departed, shouting: "Allons! Adieu! Till next Sunday!"

And as long as they could see her at all, they followed with their eyes her tall silhouette, which withdrew itself, growing smaller and smaller, and seeming to sink into the verdure of the fields.

.

When they were leaving the barracks the week after, Jean said to Luc:

"Oughtn't we to buy her something good?"

And they remained in great embarrassment before the problem of the choice of a delicacy for the girl with the cow.

Luc was of the opinion that a bit of tripe would be the best, but Jean preferred some *berlingots*, because he was fond of sweets. His choice fairly made him enthusiastic, and they bought at a grocer's two sous' worth of candies white and red.

They ate their breakfast more rapidly than usual, being nervous with expectation.

Jean saw her the first. "There she is!" said he. Luc continued: "Yes, there she is."

While yet some distance off she laughed at seeing them. She cried:

"Is everything going as you like it?"

They answered together:

"Are you getting on all right?"

Then she conversed, talked to them of simple things in which they felt an interest —of the weather, of the crops, and of her master.

They were afraid to offer her their candies, which were slowly melting away in Jean's pocket.

At last Luc grew bold, and murmured:

"We have brought you something."

She demanded, "What is it? Tell me!"

Then Jean, blushing up to his ears, managed to get at the little paper cornucopia, and held it out.

She began to eat the little pieces of sugar, rolling them from one cheek to the other. And they made lumps beneath her flesh. The two soldiers, seated before her, regarded her with emotion and delight.

Then she went to milk her cow, and once more gave them some milk on coming back.

They thought of her all the week; several times they even spoke of her. The next Sunday she sat down with them for a little longer talk; and all three, seated side by side, their eyes lost in the distance, clasping their knees with their hands, told the small doings, the minute details of their life in the villages where they had been born, while over there the cow, seeing that the milk-maid had stopped on her way, stretched out towards her its heavy head with the dripping nostrils, and gave a long low to call her back.

Soon the girl consented to eat a bit of bread with them and drink a mouthful of wine. She often brought them plums in her pocket; for the season of plums had come. Her presence sharpened the wits of the two little Breton soldiers, and they chattered like two birds.

But, one Tuesday, Luc le Ganidec asked for leave—a thing which had never happened before—and he did not return until ten o'clock at night.

Jean racked his brains uneasily for a reason for his comrade's going out in this way.

The next Thursday Luc, having borrowed ten sous from his bed-fellow, again asked and obtained permission to leave the barracks for several hours.

And when he set off with Jean on their Sunday walk his manner was very queer, quite restless and quite changed. Kerderen did not understand, but he vaguely suspected something without divining what it could be.

They did not say a word to one another until they reached their usual stopping-place, where, from their constant sitting in the same spot, the grass was quite worn away. And they ate their breakfast slowly. Neither of them felt hungry.

Before long the girl appeared. As on every Sunday, they watched her coming. When she was quite near, Luc rose and made two steps forward. She put her milk-pail on the ground, and kissed him. She kissed him passionately, throwing her arms about his neck, without noticing Jean, without remembering that he was there, without even seeing him.

And he sat there desperate, he the poor Jean, so desperate that he did not understand, his soul quite overwhelmed, his heart bursting, not yet expressing it all to himself.

Then the girl seated herself beside Luc, and they began to chatter.

Jean did not look at them: he now divined why his comrade had gone out twice during the week, and he felt within him a burning grief, a kind of wound, that sense of rending which is caused by a treason.

Luc and the girl got up together to go and change the position of the cow.

Jean followed them with his eyes. He saw them departing side by side. The red breeches of his comrade made a bright spot on the road. It was Luc who picked up the mallet and hammered down the stake to which they tied the beast.

The girl stooped to milk her, while he stroked the cow's sharp spine with a careless hand. Then they left the milk-pail on the grass, and they went deep into the wood.

Jean saw nothing more but the wall of leaves where they had entered; and he felt himself so troubled that if he had tried to rise he would certainly have fallen.

He sat motionless, stupefied by astonishment and suffering, by a suffering which was simple but which was deep. He wanted to cry, to run away, to hide himself, never to see anybody any more.

Suddenly he saw them issuing from the thicket. They returned gently, holding each other's hands, as in the villages do those who are promised. It was Luc who carried the pail.

They kissed one another again before they separated, and the girl went off after having thrown Jean a friendly "good-evening" and a smile which was full of meaning. To-day she no longer thought of offering him any milk.

The two little soldiers sat side by side, motionless as usual, silent and calm, their placid faces betraying nothing of all which troubled their hearts. The sun fell on them. Sometimes the cow lowed, looking at them from afar.

At their usual hour they rose to go back.

Luc cut a switch. Jean carried the empty bottle. He returned it to the wine-seller at Bezons. Then they sallied out upon the bridge, and, as they did every Sunday, they stopped several minutes in the middle to watch the water flowing.

Jean leaned, leaned more and more, over the iron railing, as though he saw in the current something which attracted him. Luc said: "Are you trying to drink?" Just as he uttered the last word Jean's head overbalanced his body, his legs described a circle in the air, and the little blue and red soldier fell in a lump, entered the water, and disappeared.

Luc, his throat paralyzed with anguish, tried in vain to shout. Farther down he saw something stir; then the head of his comrade rose to the surface of the river and re-entered it as soon.

Farther still he again perceived a hand, a single hand which issued from the stream and then plunged back. That was all.

The barge-men who ran up did not find the body that day.

Luc returned alone to the barracks, running, his head filled with madness; and he told of the accident, with tears in his eyes and voice, blowing his nose again and again: "He leaned over ... he ... he leaned over ... so far ... so far that his head turned a somersault; and ... and ... so he fell ... he fell. ..."

He was strangled by emotion, he could say no more. If he had only known!

XIII.
THE WRECK.

THE WRECK.

It was yesterday, the 31st of December.

I had just finished breakfast with my old friend Georges Garin when the servant brought him in a letter covered with seals and foreign stamps.

Georges said:

"Will you excuse me?"

"Certainly."

And so he began to read eight pages in a large English handwriting, crossed in every direction. He read them slowly, with serious attention and the interest which we only pay to things which touch our hearts.

Then he put the letter on a corner of the mantle-piece, and he said:

"'That was a curious story! I've never

told you about it, I think. And yet it was a sentimental adventure, and it happened to me. Aha! That was a strange New-year's Day indeed! It must be twenty years ago, since I was then thirty, and am now fifty years old.

"I was then an inspector in the Maritime Insurance Company, of which I am now director. I had arranged to pass the fête of New-year's in Paris—since it is a convention to make that day a fête—when I received a letter from the manager, directing me to proceed at once to the island of Ré, where a three-masted vessel from Saint-Nazaire, insured by us, had just gone ashore. It was then eight o'clock in the morning. I arrived at the office at ten, to get my instructions · and the same evening I took the express, which put me down in La Rochelle the next day, December 31st.

"I had two hours to spare before going aboard the boat for Ré. So I made a tour in the town. It is certainly a fantastic city, La Rochelle, with a strong character of its own—streets tangled like a labyrinth, sidewalks running under endless arcaded galleries like those of the Rue de Rivoli, but low, mysterious, built as if to form a fit scene for conspirators, and making an ancient and striking background for those old-time wars, the savage heroic wars of religion. It is indeed the typical old Huguenot city, grave, discreet, with no fine art to show, with no wonderful monuments, such as make Rouen so grand; but it is remarkable for its severe, somewhat cunning look; it is a city of obstinate fighters, a city where fanaticisms might well blossom, where the faith of the Calvinists became exalted, and where the plot of the 'Four Sergeants' was born.

"After I had wandered for some time about these curious streets, I went aboard the black, fat-bellied little steamboat which was to take me to the island of Ré. It was called the *Jean Guiton*. It started with angry puffings, passed between the two old towers which guard the harbor, crossed the roadstead, and issued from the mole built by Richelieu, the great stones of which are visible at the water's edge, enclosing the town like an immense necklace. Then the steamboat turned off to the right.

"It was one of those sad days which oppress and crush the thoughts, tighten the heart, and extinguish in us all energy and force—a gray, icy day, salted by a heavy mist which was as wet as rain, as cold as frost, as bad to breathe as the lye of a wash-tub.

"Under this low ceiling of sinister fog, the shallow, yellow, sandy sea of all gradually receding coasts lay without a wrinkle, without a movement, without life, a sea of turbid water, of greasy water, of stagnant water. The *Jean Guiton* passed over it, rolling a little from habit, dividing the smooth, opaque sheet, and leaving behind a few waves, a little chopping sea, a few undulations, which were soon calm.

"I began to talk to the captain, a little man almost without feet, as round as his boat and balancing himself like it. I wanted some details about the disaster on which I was to deliver a report. A great square-rigged three-master, the *Marie Joseph*, of Saint-Nazaire, had gone ashore one night in a hurricane on the sands of the island of Ré.

"The owner wrote us that the storm had thrown the ship so far ashore that it was impossible to float her, and that they had had to remove everything which could be detached, with the utmost possible haste. Nevertheless, I was to examine the situation of the wreck, estimate what must have been her condition before the disaster, and decide whether all efforts had been used to get her afloat. I came as an agent of the company in order to bear contradictory testimony, if necessary, at the trial.

"On receipt of my report, the manager would take what measures he judged necessary to protect our interests.

"The captain of the *Jean Guiton* knew all about the affair, having been summoned with his boat to assist in the attempts at salvage.

"He told me the story of the disaster, and very simply too. The *Marie Joseph*, driven by a furious gale, lost her bearings completely in the night, and steering by chance over a heavy foaming sea—'a milk-soup sea,' said the captain—had gone ashore on those immense banks of sand which make the coasts of this region seem like limitless Saharas at hours when the tide is low.

"While talking I looked around and ahead. Between the ocean and the lowering sky lay a free space where the eye could see far. We were following a coast. I asked:

"'Is that the island of Ré?'

"'Yes, sir.'

"And suddenly the captain stretched his right hand out before us, pointed to something almost invisible in the middle of the sea, and said :

"'There's your ship!'

"'The *Marie Joseph?*'

"'Yes.'

"I was stupefied. This black, almost imperceptible speck, which I should have taken for a rock, seemed at least three miles from land.

"I continued:

"'But, captain, there must be a hundred fathoms of water in that place?'

"He began to laugh.

"'A hundred fathoms, my boy! Well, I should say about two!'

"He was from Bordeaux. He continued:

"'It's now 9.40, just high tide. Go down along the beach with your hands in your pockets after you've had your lunch at the Hôtel du Dauphin, and I'll engage that at ten minutes to three, or three o'clock, you'll reach the wreck without wetting your feet, and have from an hour and three-quarters to two hours aboard of her; but not more, or you'll be caught. The farther the sea goes out the faster it comes back. This coast is as flat as a bed-bug! But start away at ten minutes to five, as I tell you, and at half-past seven you will be aboard of the *Jean Guiton* again, which will put you down this same evening on the quay at La Rochelle.'

"I thanked the captain, and I went and sat down in the bow of the steamer to get a good look at the little city of Saint-Martin, which we were now rapidly approaching.

"It was just like all the miniature seaports which serve as the capitals of the barren islands scattered along the coast—a large fishing village, one foot on sea and one on shore, living on fish and wild-fowl, vegetables and shell-fish, radishes and mussels.

The island is very low, and little cultivated, yet seems to be filled with people. However, I did not penetrate into the interior.

"After having breakfasted, I climbed across a little promontory, and then, as the tide was rapidly falling, I started out across the sands towards a kind of black rock which I could just perceive above the surface of the water, far out, far down.

"I walked quickly over the yellow plain; it was elastic, like flesh, and seemed to sweat beneath my foot. The sea had been there very lately; now I perceived it at a distance, escaping out of sight, and I no longer distinguished the line which separated the sands from ocean. I felt as though I were assisting at a gigantic supernatural work of enchantment. The Atlantic had just now been before me, then it had disappeared into the strand, just as does scenery through a trap; and I now walked in the midst of a desert. Only the feeling, the breath of the salt-water, remained in me. I perceived the smell of the wrack, the smell of the wide sea, the rough good smell of sea-coasts. I walked fast; I was no longer cold; I looked at the stranded wreck, which grew in size as I approached, and came now to resemble an enormous shipwrecked whale.

"It seemed fairly to rise out of the ground, and on that great, flat, yellow stretch of sand assumed surprising proportions. After an hour's walk I reached it at last. Bulging out and crushed, it lay upon its side, which, like the flanks of an animal, displayed its broken bones, its bones of tarry wood pierced with enormous bolts. The sand had already invaded it, entered it by all the crannies, and held it, possessed it, refused to let it go. It seemed to have taken root in it. The bow had entered deep into this soft, treacherous beach; while the stern, high in air, seemed to cast at heaven, like a cry of despairing appeal, the two white words on the black planking, *Marie Joseph*.

"I scaled this carcass of a ship by the lowest side; then, having reached the deck, I went below. The daylight, which entered by the stove-in hatches and the cracks in the sides, showed sadly enough a species of long sombre cellar full of demolished woodwork. There was nothing here but the sand, which served as foot-soil in this cavern of planks.

"I began to take some notes about the condition of the ship. I was seated on a broken empty cask, writing by the light of a great crack, through which I could perceive the boundless stretch of the strand. A strange shivering of cold and loneliness ran over my skin from time to time; and I would often stop writing for a moment to listen to the vague mysterious noises in the wreck: the noise of the crabs scratching the planking with their hooked claws; the noise of a thousand little creatures of the sea already installed on this dead body; the noise, so gentle and regular, of the worms, who, with their gimlet-like, grinding sound, gnaw ceaselessly at the old timber, which they hollow out and devour.

"And, suddenly, very near me, I heard human voices; I started as though I had seen a ghost. For a second I really thought I was about to see two drowned men rise from the sinister depths of the hold, who would tell me about their death. At any rate, it did not take me long to swing myself on deck with all the strength I had in my wrists. There, below the bow, I found standing a tall gentleman with three young girls, or rather a tall Englishman with three young misses. Certainly, they were a good deal more frightened at seeing this sudden apparition on the abandoned three-master than I had been at seeing them. The youngest girl turned round and ran; the two others caught their father by the arms; as for him, he opened his mouth—that was sole sign of his emotion which he showed.

"Then, after several seconds, he spoke:

"'Aw, *môsieu*, are you the owner of this ship?'

"'I am.'

"'May I go over it?'

"'You may.'

"Then he uttered a long sentence in English, in which I only distinguished the word 'gracious,' repeated several times.

"As he was looking for a place to climb up, I showed him the best, and lent him a hand. He ascended. Then we helped up the three little girls, who were now quite reassured.

They were charming, especially the oldest, a blonde of eighteen, fresh as a flower, and so dainty, so pretty! Ah yes! the pretty Englishwomen have indeed the look of tender fruits of the sea. One would have said of this one that she had just risen from the sands and that her hair had kept their tint. They all, with their exquisite freshness, make you think of the delicate colors of pink sea-shells, and of shining pearls rare and mysterious, hidden in the unknown deeps of ocean.

"She spoke French a little better than her father, and she acted as interpreter. I must tell all about the shipwreck, to the very least details, and I romanced as though I had been present at the catastrophe. Then the whole family descended into the interior of the wreck. As soon as they had penetrated into this sombre, dim-lit gallery, they uttered cries of astonishment and admiration. And suddenly the father and his three daughters were holding sketch-books in their hands, which they had doubtless carried hidden somewhere in their heavy weather-proof clothes, and were all beginning at once to make pencil sketches of this melancholy and fantastic place.

"They had seated themselves side by side on a projecting beam, and the four sketch-books on the eight knees were being rapidly covered with little black lines which were intended to represent the half-opened stomach of the *Marie Joseph*.

"I continued to inspect the skeleton of the ship, and the oldest girl talked to me while she worked.

"I learned that they were spending the winter at Biarritz, and that they had come to the island of Ré expressly to see the stranded three-master. They had none of the usual English arrogance; they were simple honest hearts of that class of constant wanderers with which England covers the globe. The father was long and thin, with a red face framed in white whiskers, and looking like a living sandwich, a slice of ham cut in the shape of a head, placed between two wedges of hair. The daughters, like little wading-birds in embryo, had long legs and were also thin — except the oldest. All three were pretty, especially the tallest.

"She had such a droll way of speaking, of talking, of laughing, of understanding and of not understanding, of raising her eyes to ask a question (eyes blue as deep water), of stopping her drawing a moment to make a guess at what you meant, of returning once more to work, of saying 'yes' or 'no'—that I could have listened and looked indefinitely.

"Suddenly she murmured:

"'I hear a little movement on this boat.'

"I lent an ear; and I immediately distinguished a low, steady, curious sound. What was it? I rose and looked out of the crack, and I uttered a violent cry. The sea had come back; it was about to surround us!

"We were on deck in an instant. It was too late. The water circled us about, and was running towards the coast with prodigious swiftness. No, it did not run, it slipped, it crawled, it grew longer, like a kind of great limitless blot. The water on the sands was barely a few centimetres deep; but the rising flood had gone so far that we no longer saw the flying line of its edge.

"The Englishman wanted to jump. I

held him back. Flight was impossible because of the deep places which we had been obliged to go round on our way out, and into which we should certainly fall on our return.

"There was a minute of horrible anguish in our hearts. Then the little English girl began to smile, and murmured:

"'So we too are shipwrecked.'

"I tried to laugh; but fear caught me tight, a fear which was cowardly and horrid and base and mean, like the tide. All the dangers which we ran appeared to me at once. I wanted to shriek 'Help!' But to whom?

"The two younger girls were cowering against their father, who regarded, with a look of consternation, the measureless sea which hedged us round about.

"And the night fell as swiftly as the ocean rose—a lowering, wet, icy night.

"I said:

"'There's nothing to do but to stay on the ship.'

"The Englishman answered:

"'Oh yes!'

"And we waited there a quarter of an hour, half an hour, indeed I don't know how long, watching that yellow water which grew deep about us, whirled round and round, and seemed to bubble, and seemed to sport over the reconquest of the vast sea-strand.

"One of the little girls was cold, and we suddenly thought of going below to shelter ourselves from the light but freezing wind which blew upon us and pricked our skins.

"I leaned over the hatchway. The ship was full of water. So we must cower against the stern planking, which shielded us a little.

"The shades were now inwrapping us, and we remained pressed close to one another, surrounded by the darkness and by the sea. I felt trembling against my shoulder the shoulder of the little English girl, whose teeth chattered from time to time. But I also felt the gentle warmth of her body through her ulster, and that warmth was as delicious to me as a kiss. We no longer spoke; we sat motionless, mute, cowering down like animals in a ditch when a hurricane is raging. And, nevertheless, despite the night, despite the terrible and increasing danger, I began to feel happy that I was there, to be glad of the cold and the peril, to rejoice in the long hours of darkness and anguish which I must pass on this plank so near this dainty and pretty little girl.

"I asked myself, 'Why this strange sensation of well-being and of joy?'

"Why! Does one know? Because she was there? Who? She, a little unknown English girl? I did not love her, I did not even know her. And for all that I was touched and conquered. I should have liked to save her, to sacrifice myself for her, to commit a thousand follies! Strange thing! How does it happen that the presence of a woman overwhelms us so? Is it the power of her grace, which infolds us? Is it the seduction in her beauty and youth, which intoxicates us like wine?

"Is it not rather, as it were, the touch of Love, of Love the Mysterious, who seeks constantly to unite two beings, who tries his strength the instant he has put a man and a woman face to face, and who suffuses them with a confused, secret, profound emotion just as you water the earth to make the flowers spring?

"But the silence of the shades and of the sky became dreadful, because we could thus hear vaguely about us an infinite low roar, the dull rumor of the rising sea, and the monotonous dashing of the current against the ship.

"Suddenly I heard the sound of sobs. The youngest of the little girls was crying. Then her father tried to console her, and they began to talk in their own tongue, which I did not understand. I guessed that he was reassuring her, and that she was still afraid.

"I asked my neighbor:

"'You are not too cold, are you, miss?'

"'Oh yes. I am very cold.'

"I wanted to give her my cloak; she refused it. But I had taken it off, and I covered her with it against her will. In the short struggle her hand touched mine. It made a charming shiver run over my body.

"For some minutes the air had been growing brisker, the dashing of the water stronger against the flanks of the ship. I raised myself; a great gust blew in my face. The wind was rising!

"The Englishman perceived this at the same time that I did, and said, simply:

"'That is bad for us, this —'

"Of course it was bad, it was certain death if any breakers, however feeble, should attack and shake the wreck, which was already so loose and broken that the first big sea would carry it off in a jelly.

"So our anguish increased from second to second as the squalls grew stronger and stronger. Now the sea broke a little, and I saw in the darkness white lines appearing and disappearing, which were lines of foam; while each wave struck the *Marie Joseph*, and shook her with a short quiver which rose to our hearts.

"The English girl was trembling; I felt her shiver against me. And I had a wild desire to take her in my arms.

"Down there before and behind us, to left and right, light-houses were shining along the shore — light-houses white and yellow and red, revolving like the enormous eyes of giants who were staring at us, watching us, waiting eagerly for us to disappear. One of them in especial irritated me. It went out every thirty seconds and it lit up again as soon. It was indeed an eye, that one, with its lid ceaselessly lowered over its fiery look.

"From time to time the Englishman struck a match to see the hour; then he put his watch back in his pocket. Suddenly he said to me, over the heads of his daughters, with a gravity which was supreme:

"'I wish you a Happy New Year, *môsieu.*'

"It was midnight. I held out my hand, which he pressed. Then he said something in English, and suddenly he and his daughters began to sing 'God save the Queen,' which rose through the black and silent air and vanished into space.

"At first I felt a desire to laugh; then I was seized by a strong, fantastic emotion.

"It was something sinister and superb, this chant of the shipwrecked, the condemned, something like a prayer, and also like something grander, something comparable to the ancient sublime '*Ave Cæsar morituri te salutamus.*'

"When they had finished I asked my neighbor to sing a ballad alone, a legend, anything she liked, to make us forget our terrors. She consented, and immediately her clear young voice flew off into the night. She sang something which was doubtless sad, because the notes were long drawn out, issued slowly from her mouth, and hovered, like wounded birds, above the waves.

"The sea was rising now and beating upon our wreck. As for me, I thought only of that voice. And I thought also of the sirens. If a ship had passed near by us what would the sailors have said? My troubled spirit lost itself in the dream! A siren! Was she not really a siren, this daughter of the sea, who had kept me on this worm-eaten ship, and who was soon about to go down with me deep into the waters?

"But suddenly we were all five rolling on the deck, because the *Marie Joseph* had sunk on her right side. The English girl had fallen across me, and before I knew what I was doing, thinking that my last moment was come, I had caught her in my arms and kissed her cheek, her temple, and her hair.

"The ship did not move again, and we, we also, remained motionless.

"The father said, 'Kate!' The one whom I was holding answered, 'Yes,' and made a movement to free herself. And at that moment I should have wished the ship to split in two and let me fall with her into the sea.

"The Englishman continued:

"'A little rocking; it's nothing. I have my three daughters safe.'

"Not having seen the oldest, he had thought she was lost overboard!

"I rose slowly, and suddenly I made out a light on the sea quite near us. I shouted; they answered. It was a boat sent out in search of us by the hotel-keeper, who had guessed at our imprudence.

"We were saved. I was in despair. They picked us up off our raft, and they brought us back to Saint-Martin.

"The Englishman was now rubbing his hands and murmuring:

"'A good supper! A good supper!'

"We did sup. I was not gay. I regretted the *Marie Joseph*.

"We had to separate, the next day, after much handshaking and many promises to write. They departed for Biarritz. I was not far from following them.

"I was hard hit; I wanted to ask this little girl in marriage. If we had passed eight days together, I should have done so! How weak and incomprehensible a man sometimes is!

"Two years passed without my hearing a word from them. Then I received a letter from New York. She was married, and wrote to tell me. And since then we write to each other every year, on New-year's Day. She tells me about her life, talks of her children, her sisters, never of her husband! Why? Ah! why? ... And as for me, I only talk of the *Marie Joseph*. That was perhaps the only woman I have ever loved. No—that I ever should have loved. ... Ah, well! who can tell? Facts master you. ... And then—and then—all passes. ... She must be old now; I should not know her. ... Ah! she of the by-gone time, she of the wreck! What a creature! . . . Divine! She writes me her hair is white. . . . That caused me terrible pain. . . . Ah! her yellow hair. . . . No, *my* English girl exists no longer. . . . They are sad, such things as that!

THE END.

www.ingramcontent.com/pod-product-compliance
Lightning Source LLC
Chambersburg PA
CBHW021804230426
43669CB00008B/628